L E A R N I N G

MW00768378

0

LANGUAGE CLUES
Vocabulary
Spelling
Language Skills

Study Guide
CA 16–30
Second Edition

EDL Division
Steck-Vaughn Company

ISBN 1-56260-688-3

5 6 7 8 9 PO 05 04 03 02 01

Contents

Acknowledgments

Word-Attack Skills Author

Estelle Kleinman

Dictionary entries and pronunciation guide are taken from *Thorndike Barnhart Beginning Dictionary*, Scott, Foresman and Company, Glenview, Illinois. Entries and guide may be shortened or otherwise modified.

First Edition Field Test Participants

Kay Boles
New Caney Middle School
New Caney, Texas

Dolris Patterson
E.O. Smith Junior High School
Houston, Texas

Don Gorman-Jacobs
J.H.S. 65
New York, New York

Jamesetta Seals
Albert Thomas Junior High School
Houston, Texas

To the Instructor

Introduction

The EDL Language Clues program has five major goals: to build instant recognition of high-frequency words, to provide practice in the use of context clues to discern word meaning, to provide instruction in the many ways in which language functions, to develop proficiency with word-attack skills, and to improve spelling.

The fifteen lessons in EDL Language Clues CA 16–30 form the sixth set in the instructional program for levels AA–CA. A chart showing the skills for Level CA can be found in the EDL Language Clues Lesson Plans, CA 16–30, along with detailed teaching plans for the lessons in this Study Guide.

Teacher Orientation

Before introducing students to the Language Clues program, read the Introduction to the EDL Language Clues Lesson Plans.

Student Orientation for Vocabulary and Language Skills

Follow these steps in introducing students to the lessons:

1. Give each student a copy of the Study Guide. Have the students write their names on the inside front cover.

2. Guide students through the Introduction of the *To the Student* section of this Study Guide, by reading the section aloud to the students. Refer to the appropriate parts of *How to Use This Book* as you go through steps 3 through 7.

3. Have the students turn to Part A of Lesson CA-16. Teach both sections of Part A of Lesson CA-16, using the "Instructions for Teaching Part A" outlined in the EDL Language Clues Lesson Plans CA 16–30. Show students how to check their work with the Answer Key.

4. Teach Part B of Lesson CA-16, using the "Instructions for Teaching Part B" outlined in the EDL Language Clues Lesson Plans CA 16–30. Have students check their work with the Answer Key.

5. Introduce the students to Part C of Lesson CA-16. Guide them through the exercises and the use of the Answer Key. Tell them that in later lessons they will often complete Part C on their own.

6. Introduce the students to Part D of Lesson CA-16. Guide them through the exercise and the use of the Answer Key.

7. Show students how to arrive at a score for each part of the lesson. The words they write on the lines are **not** to be counted in scoring Parts A and B. Show students how to enter their scores and the date on the Progress Chart on pages 122–123.

Student Introduction to Spelling

Spelling lessons should follow vocabulary/language lessons by at least a week so that students can assimilate the vocabulary before being held responsible for spelling the words.

Introduce students to the spelling procedures in the following way:

1. Give a trial spelling test. During the trial test, the student writes each word two or three times. Dictate each word first and have the student write the word on a spelling worksheet. Then have the student write the word a second time by copying it from the chalkboard after you have written it. Then have the student compare the two versions and check for errors. If a word is misspelled, have the student circle the incorrect letters and write the word a third time correctly.

2. Introduce students to the Spelling Words on page 82 of this Study Guide. Those who do not do well on the trial test may use this list to study the CA-16 Lesson Words further.

3. Dictate the final spelling test for Lesson CA-16, using the procedures outlined in Part C of the EDL Language Clues Lesson Plans CA 16–30. The students respond on their own paper.

4. Introduce students to the Review Words for Lesson CA-16, on page 82 in this Study Guide. Dictate these words for a review test.

Extension Activities

At the back of this book you will find an Extension Activity for each lesson that reinforces the vocabulary and language skills taught in the lesson. These Extension Activities can be used either as a follow-up activity or as a posttest immediately after the lesson has been taught, or for review and reinforcement after some time has lapsed. Extension Activities begin on page 103. The Answer Key for the Extension Activities begins on page 118.

Introduction

Welcome to the Language Clues program. This program will help you recognize words and understand their meanings as they are used in sentences. It will also help you improve your spelling.

This program is called Language Clues because it will help you to use many kinds of clues to understand what the author is saying. Some of these clues are:

- Sounding out a word to see if it is a word you know

- Reading the sentence to see if it helps you to guess a word

- Looking at the way the word ends to get extra clues to its meaning

- Noting capital letters, because they tell you where a sentence begins and which words are the names of things

- Noticing the position of the word in the sentence, which helps you to understand its meaning

- Noticing punctuation marks, which tell you where to pause, where sentences end, and when people are talking

How to Use This Book

Each lesson has two sections. The first section is on Vocabulary and Language Skills, and the second section is on Spelling. When you start a lesson, your instructor will tell you where to turn in the book.

Vocabulary and Language Skills

There are four parts in every Vocabulary and Language Skills lesson. The parts are labeled A, B, C, and D.

In Parts A and B, you will write each word on one of these lines.

When you have written a group of words, you will complete the sentences to the right of the words.

In part A, there is also a dictionary study exercise where you will practice using dictionary entries to learn about the many meanings of someof the lesson words.

CA-16

A. WORDS IN SENTENCES

1. *Say each word and write it on the line next to the number. Then complete each sentence using the words you wrote.*

plain	1. _____
built	2. _____
cattle	3. _____
cracks	4. _____
dry	5. _____
roots	6. _____
coughing	7. _____
drift	8. _____
service	9. _____
tow	10. _____
town	11. _____

a. They _____ a fence to keep the _____ from getting lost on the _____.

b. It was so hot and _____, the grass burned down to the _____ and you could see small _____ in the ground.

c. The car engine started _____ right in the middle of a snow _____ that covered the road.

d. They had to _____ my car twenty miles to the next _____ to get to a _____ station.

CHECK ON PAGE 84

DICTIONARY—ENTRIES

2. *Study the four dictionary entries below. The words in the sentences have more than one meaning. The meaning comes from the way the word is used in a sentence. Match the way the word is used in the sentence with the correct dictionary definition by writing the number of the dictionary definition in the blank before the sentence.*

1. **drift** (drift), 1 be carried along by currents of air or water: *A raft drifts if it is not steered.* 2 go along without knowing or caring where one is going: *Some people drift without a purpose in life.* 3 meaning; direction of thought: *Please explain that again; I did not quite get the drift of your words.* 4 snow or sand heaped up by the wind: *After the heavy snow there were deep drifts in the yard.* 1, 2 *verb*, 3, 4 *noun*.

a. ____ Our ship **drifted** down the river while we were sleeping.

b. ____ He likes to **drift** along without thinking about tomorrow.

c. ____ Our car was almost covered by the **drifts** of snow.

d. ____ We could hear him, but we couldn't get the **drift** of what he said.

In Parts B and C, you will learn something about the way words work. Model boxes explain the lesson skills and give examples. Your instructor will help you get started on these parts of the lesson, then you will complete the exercises yourself.

C. WORD FUNCTIONS

You often find the words **yes**, **no**, **well**, and **oh** at the beginning of sentences. In such cases, these words form part of an answer to a question, or they are used to continue a conversation. They are followed by a comma because there is a pause after they are said.

Question: Are you ready to leave?
Answers: **Well,** I guess so.
Oh, I guess so.
Yes, I guess so.
No, I guess not.

Part D of the lesson teaches you a skill that will help you learn the use of the dictionary pronunciation guide, to divide words into syllables, and to unlock longer words. There is a model box in this part, too. Your instructor may get you started on this section, or you may complete the entire exercise alone.

D. SOUNDS IN WORDS

You know that consonants usually make just one sound, while vowels can make different sounds depending on where they appear in a word. The letter **y** can act as a consonant or a vowel.
When **y** appears at the beginning of a word, it acts like a consonant and sounds like the **y** in **yes**. Say the following words out loud to hear the sound of **y** as a consonant:

year, your, young

In the middle or end of words, the letter **y** can act as a vowel. In some cases, the **y** makes a long **i** sound as in the word **my**. Say the following words out loud to hear this sound of **y**:

try, myself, why

When **a** appears just before **y**, you hear a long **a** but the **y** is silent, as in the word **may**. Look at these examples and say each word out loud:

lay, today, way

In a word with two or more parts, the **y** at the end of the word usually makes the sound of long **e**, as in the following words:

hap-py, an-gry, coun-try

Spelling

Trial Test

Make a worksheet like the one at the right. Your instructor will pronounce one of the words and use it in a sentence. Write the word in the left-hand column.

Your instructor will write the word on the chalkboard. Copy it on the middle line.

Check the way you wrote the word in the left-hand column. If you made a mistake, draw a circle around the incorrect letters and write the word correctly on the third line.

1.	eight	ate	ate
2.	bole	boll	bowl
3.	built	built	
4.	cattle	cattle	
5.			

Practice

Practice the lesson words you missed. You can do this by studying the words on pages 82–83 in this guide.

Language Clues Spelling Words

CA-16 Lesson Words	CA-18 Lesson Words	Review Words	Review Words
1. ate	1. bar	1. puppy	1. different
2. bowl	2. bare	2. dizzy	2. attractive
3. built	3. bark	3. rattle	3. beautiful
4. cattle	4. candy	4. cattle	4. breakable
5. crop	5. dock	5. manner	5. dangerous
6. destroy	6. extra	6. matter	6. experimental
7. drift	7. jail	7. teeth	7. laughable
8. dry	8. leather	8. allow	8. lonely
9. feed	9. pet	9. tall	9. national
10. plain	10. puppy	10. tree	10. northeastern
11. prairie	11. reward	11. address	11. peaceful
12. receive	12. rug	12. application	12. pleasant
13. root	13. ruin	13. written	13. suitable
14. service	14. sailor	14. message	14. southwestern
15. tow	15. shoe	15. married	15. worthless
16. town	16. spear	16. wedding	16. wonderful
17. vacation	17. swim	17. tool	
18. wheat	18. wander	18. disappoint	**CA-22 Lesson Words**
19. cracks		19. waitress	1. alley
20. coughing	**Review Words**	20. terrible	2. blanket

vii

Spelling Test

Take the test on the lesson words. Your instructor will dictate them. You will write these words on your own paper. ──────────────────▶

1. _cattle_   1. _____
2. _vacation_   2. _____
3. _town_   3 _____
4. _plain_   4 _____
5. _____   5. _____
6 _____   6 _____

Review

Study the review words for the lesson, and take the review test. The words are on pages 82–83, just after the lesson words. You will write these words on your own paper. ──────────────────▶

1. _simplest_   1. _____
2. _angrier_   2. _____
3. _dirtiest_   3 _____
4. _____   4 _____
5. _____   5. _____

Progress Chart

Count the number of answers you got right for each part of the lesson. The number of right answers goes in the blank below the word *Score*. Also put the date on the line below the word *Date*. The *Mastery Level* tells you how many answers there are in the exercise and what is a good score. Your instructor will help you keep this chart.

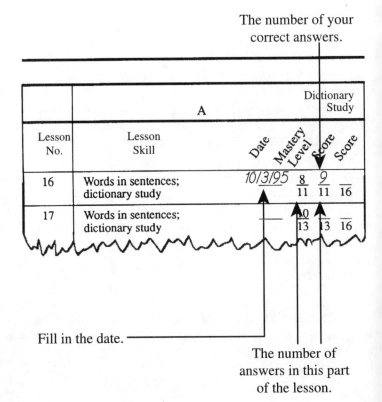

The number of your correct answers.

Lesson No.	Lesson Skill	Date	Mastery Level	Score	Dictionary Study Score
	A				
16	Words in sentences; dictionary study	10/3/95	8/11	9/11	__/16
17	Words in sentences; dictionary study	___	10/13	13	__/16

Fill in the date. ──────────

The number of answers in this part of the lesson.

A. WORDS IN SENTENCES

1. *Say each word and write it on the line next to the number. Then complete each sentence using the words you wrote.*

plain 1. _____

built 2. _____

a. They _____ a fence to keep the _____

cattle 3. _____

from getting lost on the _____.

cracks 4. _____

b. It was so hot and _____, the grass burned down to the

dry 5. _____

_____ and you could see small _____ in

roots 6. _____

the ground.

coughing 7. _____

c. The car engine started _____ right in the middle of a

drift 8. _____

snow _____ that covered the road.

service 9. _____

tow 10. _____

d. They had to _____ my car twenty miles to the next

town 11. _____

_____ to get to a _____ station.

CHECK ON PAGE 84

DICTIONARY—ENTRIES

2. *Study the four dictionary entries below. The words in the sentences have more than one meaning. The meaning comes from the way the word is used in a sentence. Match the way the word is used in the sentence with the correct dictionary definition by writing the number of the dictionary definition in the blank before the sentence.*

1. **drift** (drift), **1** be carried along by currents of air or water: *A raft drifts if it is not steered.* **2** go along without knowing or caring where one is going: *Some people drift without a purpose in life.* **3** meaning; direction of thought: *Please explain that again; I did not quite get the drift of your words.* **4** snow or sand heaped up by the wind: *After the heavy snow there were deep drifts in the yard.* **1, 2** *verb,* **3, 4** *noun.*

a. ____ Our ship **drifted** down the river while we were sleeping.

b. ____ He likes to **drift** along without thinking about tomorrow.

c. ____ Our car was almost covered by the **drifts** of snow.

d. ____ We could hear him, but we couldn't get the **drift** of what he said.

2. **plain** (plān), **1** clear; easy to understand; easily seen or heard: *The meaning is plain.* **2** without ornament or decoration; simple: *a plain dress.* **3** all of one color: *a plain blue dress.* **4** not rich or highly seasoned: *plain food.* **5** common; ordinary; simple in manner: *a plain man of the people.* **6** a flat stretch of land: *Cattle wandered over the western plains.* **1–5** *adjective,* **6** *noun.*

a. ____ She wore a **plain** black dress to the party.

b. ____ Her meaning is **plain**; she wants to go home early.

c. ____ We're just **plain** people.

d. ____ Only a few cattle moved across the empty **plain**.

1

3. **serv ice** (sėr´vis), **1** helpful act or acts; aid; being useful to others: *He performed many services for his country.* **2** supply; arrangements for supplying: *Bus service was good.* **3 services, a** performance of duties: *She no longer needs the services of a doctor.* **b** work in the service of others: *We pay for services such as repairs, maintenance, and utilities.* **4** army, navy, or air force: *My brother was in the service during the last war.* **5** a religious meeting; religious ceremony: *We attend church services twice a week. The marriage service was performed at the home of the bride.* noun.

a. _____ Train **service** is usually good on Monday.

b. _____ His brother and sister were in the **service** during the last war.

c. _____ When he got married, he wanted the **service** to be short and simple.

d. _____ What can we give for all your **services** to your country?

4. **town** (toun), **1** a large group of houses and buildings, smaller than a city: *Do you live in a town or in the country?* **2** any large place with many people living in it: *Father says Boston is a fine town.* **3** people of a town: *The whole town was having a holiday.* noun.

a. _____ We lived in a white house at the edge of **town**.

b. _____ The whole **town** went down to meet his train.

c. _____ They have one house in **town** and another one in the country.

d. _____ Johnson is a fine **town** to live in.

CHECK ON PAGE 84

B. ALPHABETICAL ORDER

In the alphabet, the letter **a** comes before the letter **b**. This is called **alphabetical order**. The words in a dictionary are placed in alphabetical order, so the word **able** comes before the word **back**.

a b c d e f g h i j k l m
able back
n o p q r s t u v w x y z
yes zoo

In the dictionary, the word **yes** comes before the word **zoo**. Why is that?

Say each word and write it on the line next to the number. Then write each word where it belongs in a sentence. Now study words 12 through 20 and write the words in alphabetical order in the blanks at the right.

ate 12. _____
receive 13. _____
destroy 14. _____
prairie 15. _____
wheat 16. _____
crop 17. _____
vacation 18. _____
Bowl 19. _____
feed 20. _____

a. Last summer, the cattle _____ all the grass on the plain.
b. Did you _____ the picture I sent?
c. The rains will _____ the young plants.
d. The farmers have sold all their _____.
e. What _____ did you plant this spring?
f. There are no mountains on the _____.
g. There are fifty pounds of chicken _____ in that bag.
h. Part of the Great Plains was once called the "Dust _____."
i. Where did you go on your _____?

CHECK ON PAGE 84

2

C. WORD FUNCTIONS

> You often find the words **yes**, **no**, **well**, and **oh** at the beginning of sentences. In such cases, these words form part of an answer to a question, or they are used to continue a conversation. They are followed by a comma because there is a pause after they are said.
>
> Question: Are you ready to leave?
> Answers: **Well**, I guess so.
>   **Oh**, I guess so.
>   **Yes**, I guess so.
>   **No**, I guess not.

Study the group of words in the boxes at the left. Then write each word so that it completes a sentence correctly. Use each word only once.

1.
| Well, |
| Oh, |
| Now, |
| Why, |

a. Where is my silk shirt?

_____ there it is.

b. You'll be sorry for that!

_____ don't get upset.

c. How do I get to West Tenth Street?

_____ you turn right at the corner, then left on the first street.

d. I don't know what to say!

_____ just say you are pleased to meet them.

2.
| Yes, |
| No, |
| Say, |
| Listen, |

a. Are you out of your mind?

_____ I'm not!

b. _____ I just heard you won the race!

c. Do you have the right time?

_____ of course I do!

d. _____ I want to ask you a few questions.

CHECK ON PAGE 84

D. SOUNDS IN WORDS

> You know that consonants usually make just one sound, while vowels can make different sounds depending on where they appear in a word. The letter **y** can act as a consonant or a vowel.
> When **y** appears at the beginning of a word, it acts like a consonant and sounds like the **y** in **yes**. Say the following words out loud to hear the sound of **y** as a consonant:
> **year, your, young**
> In the middle or end of words, the letter **y** can act as a vowel. In some cases, the **y** makes a long *i* sound as in the word **my**. Say the following words out loud to hear this sound of **y**:
> **try, myself, why**
> When **a** appears just before **y**, you hear a long **a** but the **y** is silent, as in the word **may**. Look at these examples and say each word out loud:
> **lay, today, way**
> In a word with two or more parts, the **y** at the end of the word usually makes the sound of long **e**, as in the following words:
> **hap-py, an-gry, coun-try**

3

CA-16

1. *Complete each sentence with the word that has the sound of* **y** *as in* **yes**.

    a. I haven't seen him _____.
    hurry   yet

    b. Did you go to the movies _____?
    yourself   today

    c. She gave a _____.
    party   yell

2. *Complete each sentence with the word that has the sound of* **y** *as in* **my**.

    a. Are the clothes _____?
    dry   dirty

    b. Did you see the _____?
    enemy   fly

    c. Look at the _____.
    runway   sky

3. *Complete each sentence with the word that has the sound of* **y** *as in* **may**.

    a. The ship is _____.
    steady   gray

    b. I saw the children _____.
    play   cry

    c. They exited the _____.
    subway   agency

4. *Complete each sentence with the word that has the sound of* **y** *as in* **happy**.

    a. This is a good _____.
    factory   year

    b. He has something to _____.
    bury   say

    c. It is your _____.
    pay   duty

CHECK ON PAGE 84

A. WORDS IN SENTENCES

1. *Say each word and write it on the line next to the number. Then complete each sentence using the words you wrote.*

cloth   1. _____

bucket   2. _____

cheap   3. _____

dizzy   4. _____

baby   5. _____

tough   6. _____

guy   7. _____

stray   8. _____

surprise 9. _____

eyelid 10. _____

sharp   11. _____

rapid   12. _____

dream   13. _____

a. That _____ is very _____ because it is made out of _____.

b. The _____ looked down from the edge of the bed and felt _____.

c. That _____ standing on the corner isn't as _____ as he thinks he is.

d. It was a real _____ to find the _____ cattle so quickly.

e. The cut came from something _____ that just missed her _____.

f. There are _____ eye movements when people _____.

CHECK ON PAGE 85

DICTIONARY—ENTRIES

2. *Now read the four dictionary entries below. The words in these entries have more than one meaning. The meaning of the word depends on how it is used in a sentence. Match the way the word is used in the sentence with the correct dictionary definition by writing the number of the dictionary definition in the blank before the sentence.*

1. **cheap** (chēp), **1** costing little: *Eggs are cheap now.* **2** costing less than it is worth: *My new sweater will be cheap, because my mother bought the yarn and will knit it herself.* **3** charging low prices: *He bought that suit at a very cheap department store.* **4** easily obtained: *He thinks that the cheapest way to make friends is to give them presents.* **5** common; of low value: *cheap entertainment.* *adjective.*

a. ____ Fresh fruit is not **cheap** anymore.

b. ____ The CD was **cheap** because he got it on sale.

c. ____ Flying may be the **cheapest** way to get there.

d. ____ I know from the looks of the furniture that it is not a **cheap** store.

5

2. **sharp** (shärp),   **1** having a thin cutting edge or a fine point: *a sharp knife.*   **2** having a point; not rounded: *a sharp corner on a box.*   **3** with a sudden change of direction: *a sharp turn.*   **4** feeling somewhat like a cut or prick; acting keenly on the senses: *a sharp taste, a sharp pain.*   **5** clear; distinct: *the sharp contrast between black and white.*   **6** fierce; violent: *a sharp struggle.*   **7** keen; eager: *a sharp appetite.*   **8** quick in mind; shrewd; clever: *a sharp lawyer.*   **9** promptly; exactly: *Come at one o'clock sharp.* **1–8** *adjective,* **9** *adverb.*

a. _____ Only one edge of the knife is **sharp**.

b. _____ A **sharp** operator like that will always have money to spend.

c. _____ Call me at ten o'clock **sharp**.

d. _____ After he fell, there was a **sharp** pain in his leg.

3. **sur prise** (sər priz´),   **1** feeling caused by something happening suddenly or unexpectedly: *His face showed surprise at the news.*   **2** cause to feel surprise; astonish: *The victory surprised us.*   **3** something unexpected: *Mother always has a surprise for the children on holidays.*   **4** surprising; that is not expected; coming as a surprise: *a surprise party, a surprise visit.*   **5** catch unprepared; come upon suddenly: *Our army surprised the enemy while they were sleeping.* **1, 3** *noun,* **2, 5** *verb,* **4** *adjective.*

a. _____ We gave them a **surprise** party last night.

b. _____ After dinner, we are having a **surprise**.

c. _____ You could see her **surprise** when she learned she was on TV.

d. _____ We hid in the dark and **surprised** them when they came in.

4. **tough** (tuf),   **1** bending without breaking: *Leather is tough; cardboard is not.*   **2** hard to cut, tear, or chew: *The steak was so tough he couldn't eat it.*   **3** strong; hardy: *a tough plant. Donkeys are tough little animals and can carry big loads.*   **4** hard; difficult: *Dragging the load uphill was tough work for the horses.*   **5** hard to influence; stubborn: *a tough customer.*   **6** rough; disorderly: *He lived in a tough neighborhood.*   **7** a rough person: *A gang of toughs attacked the police officer.* **1–6** *adjective,* **7** *noun.*

a. _____ That was a **tough** question, but I know the answer.

b. _____ He's not a **tough** man, but I know he can do it!

c. _____ The meat was cooked so long that it was as **tough** as animal hide.

d. _____ It was a **tough** prison, and the man was afraid.

CHECK ON PAGE 85

B. SENTENCE PATTERNS

Sentences that give information are called **statements**. All **statements** begin with a capital letter and end with a period.

capital letter → [T]he cattle destroyed the crops on the prairie [.] ← *period*

Sentences that ask something are called **questions**. All **questions** begin with a capital letter and end with a question mark.

capital letter → [H]as the tow truck come from the service station [?] ← *question mark*

Sentences that show strong feeling are called **exclamations**. All **exclamations** begin with a capital letter and end with an exclamation mark.

capital letter → [W]hat a wonderful vacation this is [!] ← *exclamation mark*

Sentences that order someone to do something are called **commands**. **Commands** may end with a period or with an exclamation mark. Most **commands** begin with a verb. The subject of a **command** is understood to be **you**.

verb → [Read] both sentences before answering the question [.] ← *period or exclamation mark*

Say each word and write it on the line next to the number. Then complete each sentence with the words you wrote.

motor 14. _____

lemon. 15. _____

Check 16. _____

Where 17. _____

hood? 18. _____

dent 19. _____

money! 20. _____

waste 21. _____

vehicle 22. _____

windows 23. _____

rattle. 24. _____

forty 25. _____

a. _____ the _____ before you buy, or you

may find that you have bought a _____

b. _____ did you get that big _____ in your

_____

c. Trying to fix up a _____ like this is a _____

of time and _____

d. At _____ miles an hour, the _____ and

doors on the truck began to _____

CHECK ON PAGE 85

C. WORD FUNCTIONS

> When you are reading, you will see three ways to say "no" with the word **not**.
> 1. Before adjectives or noun markers:
>   Those are **not** cheap jeans!
> 2. After helping verbs and before verbs:
>   The boys are **not** running today.
> 3. As part of a contraction with a helping verb:
>   Is**n't** he joining us later?
>   We could**n't** offer any more than that.

Choose one of the words from the box to complete each sentence. You may use a word more than once, and not all words will be used.

Aren't	not	no	wouldn't	Doesn't	can't	won't	isn't

a. _____ she want to hear about my experiment?

b. She did _____ understand what you said about your experiment.

c. I _____ think of anything else to say.

d. I would like to leave now, _____ you?

e. There are _____ any shirts here that I like.

f. _____ you going to fasten the rope to the boat?

CHECK ON PAGE 85

D. SYLLABICATION

The parts a word has are called **syllables**. Each syllable has only one vowel sound. Take for example the word **face**. This word has two vowels, but only one vowel sound because the **e** is silent. So this word has only one syllable.

How many vowel sounds are there in the word **forget**? There are two vowel sounds since the two vowels are both pronounced. So the word **for-get** has two syllables with one vowel sound in each syllable.

Read the following words and listen to the number of vowel sounds in each. This will be the number of syllables in the word.

One vowel sound One syllable	Two vowel sounds Two syllables	Three vowel sounds Three syllables
date	**air-port**	**di-plo-ma**
run	**car-ry**	**af-ter-noon**
arm	**win-ter**	**won-der-ful**

Write the number of parts each word has on the line.

1. ___ cheap

2. ___ eyelid

3. ___ dizzy

4. ___ vacation

5. ___ stray

6. ___ employment

7. ___ tough

8. ___ baby

9. ___ surprise

10. ___ furniture

CHECK ON PAGE 85

A. WORDS IN SENTENCES

1. *Say each word and write it on the line next to the number. Then complete each sentence using the words you wrote.*

bare 1. _____

rug   2. _____

a. When they rolled up the _____ , the _____ floor looked clean and new.

pet   3. _____

reward 4. _____

b. Mrs. James said she would pay a _____ to anyone who found her _____ cat.

extra 5. _____

bars 6. _____

jail 7. _____

c. There is an _____ amount of _____ on the windows of that _____.

dock 8. _____

sailor 9. _____

wandered 10. _____

d. The _____ had no place to go, so he _____ along the _____ where his ship was waiting.

swim 11. _____

spear 12. _____

e. Jack took a _____ each time he went for a _____ in case he wanted to hunt for fish.

CHECK ON PAGE 86

DICTIONARY ENTRIES

2. *Read the four dictionary entries below. The words in these entries have more than one meaning. The meaning depends on the way a word is used in the sentence. Match the way the word is used in the sentence with the correct dictionary definition by writing the number of the dictionary definition in the blank before the sentence.*

1. **dock** (dok), **1** platform built on the shore or out from the shore; wharf; pier. *Ships load and unload beside a dock.* **2** bring (a ship) to dock: *The sailors docked the ship and began to unload it.* **3** cut some off of: *The company docked the men's wages if they came to work late.* **4** cut short; cut off the end of. *Dogs' tails are sometimes docked.*
1 *noun,* **2–4** *verb.*

a. _____ I was **docked** fifty cents for coming in late.

b. _____ There was no room at the **dock** for our ship to land.

c. _____ After we **docked**, I had to unload the food from the ship.

d. _____ Our new boxer puppy is going to have his tail **docked**.

2. **pet** (pet), **1** animal kept as a favorite and treated with affection. **2** treated as a pet: *That girl has a pet rabbit.* **3** treat as a pet; stroke or pat; touch lovingly and gently: *She is petting the kitten.* **4** darling or favorite: *teacher's pet.* **1**, **4** *noun*, **2** *adjective*, **3** *verb*, **pet ted**, **pet ting**.

a. _____ Please feed my **pet** dog.

b. _____ I don't think she's teacher's **pet**.

c. _____ She **petted** the horse on its nose.

d. _____ Let's look in the window of the **pet** store.

3. **spear** (spir), **1** weapon with a long shaft and a sharp-pointed head. **2** pierce with a spear: *The Indian speared a fish.* **3** pierce or stab with anything sharp: *spear string beans with a fork.* **4** sprout or shoot of a plant: *a spear of grass.* **1**, **4** *noun*, **2**, **3** *verb*.

a. _____ Years ago, most natives fished with **spears**.

b. _____ The bird **speared** a fish with its sharp bill.

c. _____ There wasn't a **spear** of grass standing after the fire.

d. _____ We took a sharp stick and started to **spear** the paper that covered the ground.

4. **wan der** (won´dər), **1** move here and there without any special purpose: *We wandered through the stores, hoping to get ideas for Mother's Day presents.* **2** go from the right way; stray: *The dog wandered off and got lost. She wanders away from her subject when she talks.* **3** not be able to think sensibly: *His mind wandered when he had a very high fever.* *verb.*

a. _____ We **wandered** along the beach without knowing where we were going.

b. _____ Stay close to your mother; if you **wander** off, you'll get lost.

c. _____ When she was tired, her mind **wandered** off and she forgot what she was saying.

d. _____ The brook **wandered** slowly along until it reached the sea.

CHECK ON PAGE 86

B. SUFFIXES

The ending **ish** can give the meaning **like** when it is added to the end of a word.
If you act like a **baby**, people will say you are **babyish**.
The little **girl** gave me a sweet, **girlish** smile.

Say each word and write it on the line next to the number. Then complete each sentence using the words you wrote.

reddish 13. _____

bark 14. _____

candy 15. _____

childish 16. _____

purplish 17. _____

leather 18. _____

a. The _____ of the redwood tree is a _____ color.

b. He asked for more _____ in a high, _____ voice.

c. The lights at night gave his _____ coat a _____ look.

puppy 19. _____   d. The little _____ jumped up on us in a

puppyish 20. _____   _____ manner.

foolish 21. _____   e. You will _____ our business if you keep spending money

ruin 22. _____   in such a _____ way.

shoes 23. _____

brownish 24. _____   f. Her new _____ were a dark _____ color.

CHECK ON PAGE 86

C. WORD FUNCTIONS

> If a sentence begins with **who**, **what**, **when**, **where**, **which**, **how**, or **why**, the sentence will ask a question. These words are called **question markers** when they appear at the beginning of a question.
>
> **Who** is coming to the party?
> **What** are we going to have to eat?
> **When** will it be?
> **Where** will it be held?
> **Which** car will we go in?
> **How** will you cook the chicken?
> **Why** didn't you ask Laura?

Read the question markers in the box. Then write one question marker in the blank in each sentence. One will not be used.

| Who | When | What | Where | Which | How | Why |

a. _____ is swimming so far out in the ocean?

b. _____ will they come back to the beach?

c. _____ did they take their spears with them?

d. _____ kind of fish are they hunting?

e. _____ did they learn to fish with spears?

f. _____ will they put the fish they catch?

CHECK ON PAGE 86

11

D. SYLLABICATION

> When a word has two vowel sounds and two like consonants together in the middle, divide the word into syllables between the consonants, as in these words:
>
> **les-son, hap-py, dol-lar**
>
> When a word has two vowel sounds and two different consonants together in the middle, divide the word between the two consonants, as in the following words:
>
> **bas-ket, num-ber, prob-lem**

1. *Each of the following words has two like consonants together in the middle of the word. Divide each word into syllables and write the divided word on the blank line. One has been done for you.*

   a. cattle   *cat tle* _____

   b. puppy _____

   c. allow _____

   d. marry _____

   e. rattle _____

   f. suffer _____

   g. written _____

   h. address _____

   i. matter _____

   j. rubber _____

2. *Each of the following words has two unlike consonants together in the middle of the word. Divide each word into syllables and write the divided word on the blank line.*

   a. wander _____

   b. captain _____

   c. cancer _____

   d. slender _____

   e. powder _____

   f. platform _____

   g. control _____

   h. admit _____

   i. certain _____

   j. person _____

CHECK ON PAGE 86

A. WORDS IN SENTENCES

1. *Say each word and write it on the line next to the number. Then complete each sentence using the words you wrote.*

pressure 1. _____

mouse 2. _____

trap 3. _____

a. The _____ will spring at the smallest amount of _____ and catch another _____.

crack 4. _____

kneel 5. _____

bottom 6. _____

b. Please _____ down and tell me if you can see what's at the _____ of this _____ in the floor.

rifle 7. _____

warn 8. _____

c. If someone is coming, fire one shot from the _____ to _____ me.

wound 9. _____

lend 10. _____

d. Can you _____ me some cloth to tie up this _____?

CHECK ON PAGE 87

DICTIONARY—ENTRIES

2. *Read the three dictionary entries below. You can see that most of the words have more than one meaning. The meaning of a word comes from the way it is used in a sentence. For these entries, write the number of the definition that shows the correct meaning of the word.*

1. **bot tom** (bot′əm), **1** the lowest part: *These berries at the bottom of the basket are crushed.* **2** part on which anything rests: *The bottom of that glass is wet.* **3** ground under water: *Many wrecks lie at the bottom of the sea.* **4** seat: *This chair needs a new bottom.* **5** basis; foundation; origin: *We will get to the bottom of the mystery.* *noun.*

a. _____ The children could just reach the **bottom** leaves of that tree.

b. _____ I'll keep asking questions until we get to the **bottom** of this.

c. _____ The gold is waiting for us at the **bottom** of the sea.

d. _____ The **bottom** of the chair is broken.

2. **crack** (krak), **1** split or opening made by breaking without separating into parts: *There is a crack in this cup.* **2** break without separating into parts: *You have cracked the window.* **3** a sudden, sharp noise like that made by loud thunder, by a whip, or by something breaking. **4** make or cause to make a sudden, sharp noise: *to crack a whip. The whip cracked.* **5** hard, sharp blow: *The falling branch gave me a crack on the head.* **6** hit with a hard, sharp blow: *The falling branch cracked me on the head.* **1, 3, 5** *noun,* **2, 4, 6** *verb.*

a. _____ The wall of that house is covered with **cracks**.

b. _____ We took a stone and **cracked** the shells with one blow.

c. _____ There was a sharp **crack**, and the whole wall fell to the ground.

d. _____ After the storm, every window in the house was **cracked**.

13

3. **trap** (trap), **1** thing or means for catching animals. **2** trick or other means for catching someone off guard: *The police set traps to make the thief confess.* **3** catch in a trap: *The bear was trapped.* **4** set traps for animals: *Some men make their living by trapping animals for their furs.* **5** trap door. **6** bend in a pipe to catch small objects and to keep gas from backing up.
1, 2, 5, 6 *noun*, **3, 4** *verb*, **trapped, trap ping.**

a. _____ The bear's leg was broken by that **trap**.

b. _____ Don't go in there! It's a **trap**!

c. _____ We took two steps and fell through the **trap** door.

d. _____ She put some **traps** in every room in the house.

Check the best answer.

4. **wound**[1] (wünd), **1** hurt or injury caused by cutting, stabbing, shooting, or other violence rather than disease: *The man has a knife wound in his arm.* **2** injure by cutting, stabbing shooting, or other violence; hurt: *The hunter wounded the deer.* **3** any hurt or injury to feelings or reputation: *The loss of his job was a wound to his pride.* **4** injure in feelings or reputation: *His unkind words wounded her.*
1, 3 *noun*, **2, 4** *verb*.
wound[2] (wound). See **wind**[2]. *She wound the string into a tight ball. It is wound too loosely.*
verb.
wind[2] (wind), **1** move this way and that; go in a crooked way; change direction; turn: *A brook winds through the woods. We wound our way through the narrow streets.* **2** fold, wrap, or place about something: *The mother wound her arms about the child.* **3** cover with something put, wrapped, or folded around: *The man's arm is wound with bandages.* **4** roll into a ball or on a spool: *Grandma was winding yarn. Thread comes wound on spools.*
verb.

a. The cat **wound** its tail around the leg of the chair.

    Wound means   _____ injured

                                    _____ wrapped about

    Wound is pronounced   _____ **wünd**

                                      _____ **wound**

b. Anna's **wound** is healing nicely.

    Wound means   _____ hurt or injury

                                    _____ roll into a ball

    Wound is pronounced   _____ **wünd**

                                      _____ **wound**

CHECK ON PAGE 87

B. ALPHABETICAL ORDER

If you know the first few letters in a word, you can always find that word in a dictionary or other book in which the words are placed in alphabetical order.

	1st letter	2nd letter	3rd letter
able	a	b	l
about	a	b	o
above	a	b	o

The word **able** comes before the word **about**. The first two letters are the same. But the third letter is different. The *l* in **able** comes before the *o* in **about**.

Which comes first in the dictionary, **about** or **above**? **About** comes first because its fourth letter, *u*, comes before the letter *v*.

Say the words and write them on the lines. Then write the words in each group in alphabetical order. After that, complete each sentence using the words from the group.

	Words	Words in order

allow 11. _____   _____

arrive 12. _____   _____

army 13. _____   _____

adventure 14. _____   _____

action 15. _____   _____

a. I like movies with plenty of _____.

b. Climbing the mountain was a great _____.

c. I will not _____ you to go there alone.

d. Her train will _____ in less than an hour.

e. Do you think there's plenty of action in the _____?

success 16. _____   _____

suppose 17. _____   _____

suggest 18. _____   _____

sir 19. _____   _____

sixty 20. _____   _____

f. She was driving more than _____ miles an hour.

g. May I _____ that you drive more slowly?

h. I _____ that you are going to tell me I'm wrong.

i. "Yes, _____," he told the captain, "whatever you say."

j. We hope his new business will be a _____.

CHECK ON PAGE 87

C. SENTENCE PATTERNS

Sometimes, the first word you read in a question will be a **helping verb** instead of a question marker. When the first word in a sentence is a **helping verb**, you have a clue that a question will follow.

A statement can be made into a question by moving the helping verb like this:

He **has** made a mistake.

Has he made a mistake?

They **shouldn't** walk across the bridge.

Shouldn't they walk across the bridge?

She **is** going to stay in the yard.

Is she going to stay in the yard?

15

Read the complete statement. Then make a question of the statement by writing the missing words in the blanks.

a.   They will hear the shot from the rifle.

_____ they _____ from the rifle?

b.   She could help you clean out that wound.

_____ she help you _____?

c.   We should walk on the other side of the street.

_____ we _____?

d.   I wasn't ready when you shot the rifle.

_____ I _____?

e.   He has been expecting you to come today.

_____ he been expecting _____?

CHECK ON PAGE 87

D. SYLLABICATION

> When a syllable ends in a consonant, it is called a **closed syllable**. Look at an example:
>
>   **be-ing** —the second syllable is closed because it ends with the
>   consonant **g**.
>
> All of the syllables in the following words are **closed syllables** because they end with consonants:
>
>   ad-mit, him-self, writ-ten
>
> The vowel sound in a closed syllable is usually short.

Below you see words divided in syllables. Circle each closed syllable.

1.   bas ket
2.   in vent
3.   e ven
4.   a go
5.   suc cess

6.   be long
7.   hel lo
8.   sug gest
9.   ra dar
10.   de gree

CHECK ON PAGE 87

A. WORDS IN SENTENCES

1. *Say each word and write it on the line next to the number. Then complete each sentence using the words you wrote.*

ocean   1. _____

anchor   2. _____

thousand   3. _____

cheer   4. _____

bridge   5. _____

forward   6. _____

folks   7. _____

except   8. _____

disturb   9. _____

welcome   10. _____

trust   11. _____

permit   12. _____

material   13. _____

yard   14. _____

wet   15. _____

mistake   16. _____

a. The ship dropped _____ where the _____ was almost one _____ feet deep.

b. The men gave a _____ as the captain walked _____ and stood on the _____ of the ship.

c. I am sorry to _____ you, _____, but no one _____ the crew is allowed on this deck.

d. I _____ you will _____ me to _____ you home.

e. That _____ would be good for a dress, but it costs too much for a _____.

f. It would be a big _____ to touch that electric wire while your hands and feet are still _____.

CHECK ON PAGE 88

DICTIONARY—ENTRIES

2. *Read the three dictionary entries below. You can see that the words have more than one meaning. The meaning of a word comes from the way it is used in a sentence. Match the way the word is used in the sentence with the correct dictionary definition by writing the number of the dictionary definition in the blank before the sentence.*

1. **bridge** (brij),   **1** something built that carries a road, railroad, or path across a river, road, or the like.   **2** make a way over a river or anything that hinders: *The engineers bridge the river. A log bridged the brook.*   **3** platform above the deck of a ship for the officer in command: *The captain directed the course of his ship from the bridge.*   **4** the upper, bony part of the nose.
1, 3, 4 *noun,* **2** *verb,* **bridged, bridg ing.**

a. ____ The soldiers **bridged** the river in only two days.

b. ____ It costs fifty cents to drive across the new **bridge**.

c. ____ The captain stood on the **bridge** of the ship right through the storm.

d. ____ The ball struck the **bridge** of his nose and broke it.

2. **cheer** (chir),   **1** a shout of encouragement and support or praise: *Give three cheers for the boys who won the game for us.*   **2** show praise and approval by cheers: *The boys cheered loudly.*   **3** urge on with cheers: *Everyone cheered our team.*   **4** good spirits; hope; gladness: *The warmth of the fire and a good meal brought cheer to our hearts again.*   **5** give joy to; make glad; comfort: *It cheered the old woman to have us visit her.*
1, 4 *noun,* **2, 3, 5** *verb.*

a. ____ When our team won the last game, everyone **cheered**.

b. ____ She brought those flowers to **cheer** me up.

c. ____ The flowers and the music gave everyone a feeling of good **cheer**.

d. ____ Let's have three **cheers** for the winners!

3. **trust** (trust),   **1** firm belief in the honesty, truthfulness, justice, or power of a person or thing; faith: *A child puts trust in his parents.*   **2** believe firmly in the honesty, truth, justice, or power of; have faith in: *He is a man you can trust.*   **3** rely on; depend on: *A forgetful man should not trust his memory, but should write things down.*   **4** hope; believe: *I trust you will soon feel better.*   **5** commit to the care of; leave without fear: *Can I trust the keys to him?*
1 noun, **2–5** verb.

a. ____ His record shows he is a person you can **trust**.

b. ____ I can **trust** my car to Bill.

c. ____ My father puts great **trust** in his doctor.

d. ____ I **trust** you will remember our meeting tomorrow.

For the following word, the dictionary gives two pronunciations of the word and two definitions. For this entry, you will also check the correct pronunciation for the way the word is used in the sentence.

4. **per mit** (pər mit´ *for 1;* pėr´mit *for 2*),   **1** let; allow: *My mother will not permit me to stay up late. The law does not permit smoking in this store.*   **2** a formal written order giving permission to do something: *Have you a permit to fish in this lake?*
1 *verb,* **per mit ted, per mit ting; 2** *noun.*

a. ____ Will you **permit** me to stay up until midnight?

Permit is pronounced:

____ pər mit´ ____ per´mit

b. ____ Do you have a **permit** to camp in this forest?

Permit is pronounced:

____ pər mit´ ____ per´mit

CHECK ON PAGE 88

B. PREFIXES

When the prefix **re** appears before a word, it may mean "again." Sometimes there may be a **hyphen** between the **re** and the rest of the word.

　　She is going to put a new **cover** on the chair.

　　She is going to have her chair **re-covered**.

The prefix **re** may also mean "back." There is no hyphen when **re** means "back."

　　John told me, "I will **pay** you tomorrow."

　　"You can **repay** me whenever you can," I said.

Some other words like **reward** and **receive** look and sound as though they have the prefix **re** added, but the **re** does not mean "again" or "back."

*Say the words and write them in the numbered blanks below. Then choose the word that completes each sentence correctly and write it in the blank in the sentence. After that, decide what meaning the **re** has in that word, and make a check mark in the appropriate column*

17. _____
　　　respected

18. _____
　　　reelection

19. _____
　　　replace

20. _____
　　　refused

21. _____
　　　recount

22. _____
　　　rejoin

	Re means again	*Re* means back	*Re* does NOT mean again or back
a. I _____ her offer to work without pay.			
b. After the election, both people wanted to have a _____ of the vote.			
c. I have to _____ the book I lost.			
d. Sue _____ his wish to be left alone.			
e. John will _____ the other people as soon as he feels better.			
f. Mr. Counts was trying for _____, but he lost this time.			

CHECK ON PAGE 88

C. WORD FUNCTIONS

Sometimes you will see a form of the word **do** at the beginning of a question. We use the words **do**, **does**, **did**, **doesn't**, **don't**, and **didn't** to show that the sentence is a question.

statement		The anchor weighs one thousand pounds.
question	*Does*	the anchor weigh one thousand pounds?
statement		He made only one mistake.
question	*Did*	he make only one mistake?
statement		You don't want to be disturbed.
question	*Don't*	you want to be disturbed?

Read the complete statement. Then make a question out of each statement by writing the correct form of **do** *in the blank space.*

a. That material costs five dollars a yard.

_____ that material cost five dollars a yard?

b. They don't know if the bridge has been burned.

_____ they know if the bridge has been burned?

c. She didn't know the gun was loaded.

_____ she know the gun was loaded?

d. They refused to give us food.

_____ they refuse to give us food?

e. Your sister doesn't know what she's going to do.

_____ your sister know what she's going to do?

CHECK ON PAGE 88

D. SYLLABICATION

> When two consonants have one sound—as with the *th*, *ch*, or *sh* sound—do not divide the word into syllables between the two consonants.
> Note that even though two consonants appear in the middle of these two-syllable words, the words are not broken between the consonants:
> **moth-er, fath-er, teach-er, dish-es**
> Also, when a word is divided into syllables, do not separate consonant blends such as *st*, *pl*, and *tr*. The blend acts as one sound and cannot be separated, as shown in the following examples:
> **in-stead, ex-plain, con-trol**

Below each sentence are three ways that the underlined word could be broken into syllables. Circle the correct way.

1. I have some <u>extra</u> time.

   ext-ra   e-xtra   ex-tra

2. The child thought he saw a <u>monster</u>.

   mons-ter   mon-ster   mo-nster

3. He is in the <u>kitchen</u> cooking supper.

   ki-tchen   kitc-hen   kit-chen

4. What will the <u>weather</u> be like tomorrow?

   weath-er   weat-her   we-ather

5. He gave her a <u>surprise</u> party.

   surp-rise   surpr-ise   sur-prise

6. I don't get any <u>respect</u>.

   res-pect   resp-ect   re-spect

CHECK ON PAGE 88

REVIEW 16-20

Say each word and write it on the line next to the number. Then complete each part by writing one word on each blank line. The numbers under the lines tell you which words to choose from.

A.
1. _____ dream
2. _____ crop
11. _____ wet
12. _____ extra

3. _____ anchor
4. _____ eyelid
13. _____ feed
14. _____ dry

5. _____ forty
6. _____ sixty
15. _____ yard
16. _____ shoe

7. _____ mistake
8. _____ thousand
17. _____ dizzy
18. _____ welcome

9. _____ folks
10. _____ cattle
19. _____ arrive
20. _____ receive

The sound of the radio cut through Hector's _____. He opened one _____
(1 or 2)   (3 or 4)

and looked around. Everything still seemed strange. He had come to this country two months ago, and in

those _____ days he hadn't made one friend. Was it a _____ coming here? No, he
(5 or 6)   (7 or 8)

had to come. The _____ back home needed the _____ money he would send them
(9 or 10)   (11 or 12)

to _____ the family.
(13 or 14)

After weeks of looking, Hector had found a job in a _____ store. He wondered if the other
(15 or 16)

workers would make him feel _____. "I'd better not _____ late on the first day,"
(17 or 18)   (19 or 20)

he thought while looking for his shoes.

B.
21. _____ sailor
22. _____ puppy
31. _____ ruin
32. _____ wound

23. _____ stray
24. _____ mouse
33. _____ ate
34. _____ built

25. _____ army
26. _____ town
35. _____ bar
36. _____ bowl

27. _____ bucket
28. _____ pet
37. _____ lend
38. _____ destroy

29. _____ bark
30. _____ cheer
39. _____ permit
40. _____ trap

Hector laughed when he saw his _____ playing with his shoe. The dog was a
(21 or 22)

_____ he had found just one week after coming to this _____. With the
(23 or 24)   (25 or 26)

_____, he wasn't so lonely. As Hector took his shoe away from the puppy, the dog gave a
(27 or 28)

22

_____ as if to say, "Why must you _____ my fun?"
    (29 or 30)   (31 or 32)

Hector _____ quickly and put down a fresh _____ of water for his dog.
         (33 or 34)   (35 or 36)

Before leaving, he looked at her and said, "Now if you don't _____ anything, I'll
                                                              (37 or 38)

_____ you to go for a ride in my new car later."
    (39 or 40)

C.

41. _____   42. _____   51. _____   52. _____
         crack   prairie   reward   disturb

43. _____   44. _____   53. _____   54. _____
         dent   dock   rapid   cheap

45. _____   46. _____   55. _____   56. _____
         ocean   hood   vehicle   bridge

47. _____   48. _____   57. _____   58. _____
         baby   motor   bare   sharp

49. _____   50. _____   59. _____   60. _____
        rattle   rug   surprise   success

Hector's car was a wreck. One window had a long _____, and there was a big
                                                      (41 or 42)

_____ on the driver's side. Things weren't much better under the _____. The
    (43 or 44)   (45 or 46)

_____ made a _____ that would often _____ other drivers. Hector
    (47 or 48)   (49 or 50)   (51 or 52)

thought, "That's why it was so _____." Thinking about the great _____ he would
                                  (53 or 54)   (55 or 56)

buy some day, he got into his car and drove off.

Suddenly, a small white car cut Hector off. He had to make a _____ turn to keep from
                                                                 (57 or 58)

hitting it. It was a _____ to Hector to see that the driver was a young woman who had children
                        (59 or 60)

in the back of the car.

D.

61. _____   62. _____   69. _____   70. _____
       vacation   drift   warn   waste

63. _____   64. _____   71. _____   72. _____
       pressure   cloth   wander   suggest

65. _____   66. _____   73. _____   74. _____
        spear   leather   sir   guy

67. _____   68. _____
       bottom   tough

Once at the store, Hector was busy because many workers were on _____. He was a quick
                                                                    (61 or 62)

learner, who worked well under _____. While showing a man some _____
                                  (63 or 64)   (65 or 66)

shoes, he heard his boss talking to another worker.

"You're late again, Julia."

"I'm sorry, Mr. Perez. I had to drop my children off at daycare," Julia answered.

"I know things have been _____ on you since your husband died, but I must
(67 or 68)

_____ you to get here on time. I _____ you find a way to do so."
(69 or 70)   (71 or 72)

    "Yes, _____," Julia said.
(73 or 74)

    When Hector turned around, he saw that Julia was the driver who had cut him off. Now he knew why she

had been in such a hurry.

E.

75. _____   76. _____   85. _____   86. _____
     material   service   jail   coughing

77. _____   78. _____   87. _____   88. _____
     root   plain   forward   except

79. _____   80. _____   89. _____   90. _____
     wheat   lemon   action   swim

81. _____   82. _____   91. _____   92. _____
     candy   rifle   kneel   refuse

83. _____   84. _____   93. _____   94. _____
     trust   respect   suppose   tow

    "Can I get some _____ here?" a man asked of Hector. "I'd like to see these
(75 or 76)

_____ black shoes in eleven."
(77 or 78)

"I'll bring them right out," Hector answered.

As he was getting the shoes, Hector saw a bowl of hard candies. He put a _____
(79 or 80)

_____ in his mouth before going back to the man.
(81 or 82)

    "I _____ you'll find these to your liking," Hector said, showing the man the shoes.
(83 or 84)

Suddenly, Hector started _____. The candy had gotten stuck in his throat. He couldn't breathe!
(85 or 86)

    Julia came _____ and jumped into _____. Grabbing Hector around the
(87 or 88)   (89 or 90)

middle from behind, she pushed in and up with a hard fist. The candy came flying out.

    Hector couldn't thank Julia enough. "I want to buy you lunch," he told her. "Please don't

_____."
(91 or 92)

    When Julia smiled and said yes, Hector thought, "I _____ I can make friends here after all."
(93 or 94)

CHECK ON PAGE 89

A. WORDS IN SENTENCES

1. *Say each word and write it on the line next to the number. Then complete each sentence using the words you wrote.*

private   1. _____

relax   2. _____

a. "Let us talk next _____ in _____," he said,

Friday   3. _____

"when we can _____."

silence   4. _____

silent   5. _____

b. We fell _____ until the _____ began to

silly   6. _____

make us all feel _____.

shock   7. _____

students   8. _____

c. The _____ was started by a few _____ who

blaze   9. _____

wanted to _____ the country.

alcohol   10. _____

d. They said they would _____ the tables and chairs and

smash   11. _____

pour _____ over the dry wood.

dozen   12. _____

court   13. _____

e. He told the king it would take a _____ men to

repair   14. _____

_____ the damage to his _____.

fumes   15. _____

f. The _____ of alcohol will burn if anyone is

stupid   16. _____

_____ enough to light a match.

CHECK ON PAGE 90

DICTIONARY—ENTRIES

2. *Study the four dictionary entries. Write the number of the definition that tells the meaning of the word as it is used in the sentence.*

1. **court** (kôrt),   **1** space partly or wholly enclosed by walls or buildings: *The four apartment houses were built around a court of grass.*   **2** place marked off for a game: *a tennis court, a basketball court.*   **3** place where a king, emperor, or other sovereign lives; royal palace.   **4** establishment and followers of a king, emperor, or other sovereign: *The court of King Solomon was noted for its splendor.*   **5** place where justice is administered: *The prisoner was brought to court for trial.* *noun.*

a. ____ The lights made the basketball **court** as bright as day.

b. ____ Inside the building there was a small **court** with green grass and two trees.

c. ____ The king's **court** was made of stone and dark wood.

d. ____ The police officer took both men to **court**.

2. **pri vate** (prī´vit),   **1** not for the public; for just a few special people or for one: *a private road, a private house, a private letter.*   **2** not public; personal: *the private life of a king, my private opinion. A diary is a private journal.*   **3** secret: *News reached him through private channels. He put the purse in a private pocket.*   **4** having no public office: *a private citizen.*   **5** soldier or marine of the lowest rank: *His brother was promoted from private to corporal last week.*
1–4 *adjective,* **5** *noun.*

a. _____ Keep off! This is a **private** road.

b. _____ After he lost the election, he became a **private** person again.

c. _____ No one knew about Mr. Simon's **private** letters.

d. _____ General White was only a **private** when he was wounded in World War II.

3. **shock** (shok),   **1** a sudden, violent shake, blow, or crash: *Earthquake shocks are often felt in Japan. The two trains collided with a terrible shock.*   **2** a sudden, violent, or upsetting disturbance: *His death was a great shock to his family.*   **3** cause to feel surprise, horror, or disgust: *That child's bad language shocks everyone.*   **4** a collapsing or weakening of the body or mind caused by some violent impression on the nerves: *The operation was successful, but the patient suffered from shock.*   **5** disturbance produced by an electric current passing through the body.   **6** give an electric shock to.
1, 2, 4, 5 *noun,* **3, 6** *verb.*

a. _____ The mouse in that experiment was given a small **shock**.

b. _____ Billy's mistake was a **shock** to us all.

c. _____ They took her to the hospital because she was suffering from **shock**.

d. _____ After the bombs fell, there was a great **shock** that ran through the earth.

4. **smash** (smash),   **1** break into pieces with violence and noise: *The boy smashed a window with a stone.*   **2** destroy; shatter; ruin: *smash a person's hopes.*   **3** be broken to pieces: *The dishes smashed as the tray upset.*   **4** become ruined.   **5** rush violently; crash: *The car smashed into the tree.*   **6** a violent breaking; shattering; crash: *Two cars were involved in the smash.*   **7** sound of a smash or crash: *the smash of broken glass.*   **8** a crushing defeat; disaster.
1–5 *verb,* **6–8** *noun, plural* **smash es.**

a. _____ The accident **smashed** every window in the car.

b. _____ In the kitchen, we could hear the **smash** of broken dishes.

c. _____ If she loses the election, it will **smash** her hopes for success.

d. _____ Four vehicles were destroyed in the **smash**.

CHECK ON PAGE 90

B. COMPOUND WORDS

When two words are written together to make one longer word, we call it a **compound word**.
A **footprint** is a **print**, or shape, made by a **foot**.

Say each word and write it on the line next to the number. Complete each sentence with the words you wrote. Then draw a line between the two words that make up the compound words.

become 17. _____   a. Alan will _____ a _____ in his father's

foreman 18. _____   factory.

bareback 19. _____   b. It soon _____ clear that Billy was not a good

became 20. _____   _____ rider.

26

motorboat 21. _____

swimsuit 22. _____

doorway 23. _____

backyard 24. _____

aftershock 25. _____

earthquake 26. _____

touchdown 27. _____

grandstand 28. _____

fullback 29. _____

c. Put on your _____ when you go out in the

_____.

d. From the _____, you can see the flowers growing in

the _____.

e. After the _____, there was a bad _____

which damaged still more buildings.

f. Everyone in the _____ cheered when the

_____ made a _____.

CHECK ON PAGE 90

C. PREPOSITIONS

Prepositions are words that come before a noun. They work with the noun to answer the question, "**when**," "**where**," "**how**," or "**which**."

The moon comes **over** the mountain.   Answers **where**

She leaves **by** the back door.   Answers **how**

The preposition, the noun, and any words in between are sometimes called a **prepositional phrase**. A prepositional phrase can come at the beginning, in the middle, or at the end of a sentence.

Study the prepositions in the box. Then read each sentence and circle the prepositions. Draw a line under the noun and any other words that go with the preposition. On the line at the right, write what each prepositional phrase tells us: **when***,* **where***,* **how***, or* **which***.*

| after | at | before | behind | by | down | for | from |
| in | into | on | out | over | under | with |

a. In the king's court, the men and women begin working at noon.   _____

b. My brother ran down the stairs and into the hall.   _____

c. Before the party, they walked to the store.   _____

d. With an angry look, the customer smashed the glass on the table.   _____

e. The king was killed by a trick before the whole court.   _____

f. Some friends of my father's came to visit us after the football game.   _____

CHECK ON PAGE 90

D. SYLLABICATION

There is another clue that will help you divide words with more than one syllable. When the first vowel is followed by one consonant, the vowel usually ends the first syllable. The consonant begins the second syllable. Look at the following examples:

pa-per, o-pen, mu-sic

Say each word out loud. What vowel sound does the first syllable have in each word? It has the long vowel sound. In syllables ending in vowels, called **open syllables**, the vowel sound is usually long.

Divide each word into syllables. Write the divided word on the blank line.

1. student _____
2. depend _____
3. elect _____
4. became _____
5. famous _____

6. pretend _____
7. ocean _____
8. receive _____
9. stupid _____
10. motor _____

CHECK ON PAGE 90

A. WORDS IN SENTENCES

1. *Say each word and write it on the line next to the number. Then complete each sentence using the words you wrote.*

alley   1. _____

growl   2. _____

repeat   3. _____

secret   4. _____

treat   5. _____

thirsty   6. _____

blanket   7. _____

rag   8. _____

insurance   9. _____

notice   10. _____

remain   11. _____

policy   12. _____

pen   13. _____

premium   14. _____

pencil   15. _____

human   16. _____

reply   17. _____

prepare   18. _____

a. We heard a low _____ from the _____.

b. If I _____ what she said, will you keep it a _____?

c. When you're _____, cool water is a real _____.

d. The dog chewed our _____ until it was nothing more than a _____.

e. We received a _____ from the _____ company.

f. He said our _____ will _____ in force this year.

g. I took my _____ and wrote a check to pay the insurance _____.

h. With his _____, he drew a picture of a dog that looked almost _____.

i. The question was hard, so I took a long time to _____ my _____.

CHECK ON PAGE 91

DICTIONARY—ENTRIES

2. *Study the four dictionary entries on the next page. You can see that each word has more than one meaning. The meaning comes from the way each word is used in a sentence. Write the number of the definition in front of the sentence at the right that matches its meaning.*

29

1. **blan ket** (blang´kit), **1** a soft, heavy covering woven from wool, cotton, nylon, or other material, used to keep people or animals warm. **2** anything like a blanket: *A blanket of snow covered the ground.* **3** cover with a blanket: *The snow blanketed the ground.*
   1, 2 *noun,* **3** *verb.*

a. _____ The fog covered the road like a heavy, gray **blanket**.

b. _____ The heavy snow **blanketed** the driveway.

c. _____ The baby's **blanket** is light blue.

d. _____ When we went to camp we forgot our **blankets**.

2. **no tice** (nō´tis), **1** heed; attention: *A sudden movement caught his notice.* **2** see; give attention to; observe: *I noticed a hole in my stocking.* **3** information; warning: *The whistle blew to give notice that the boat was about to leave.* **4** a written or printed sign; paper posted in a public place; large sheet of paper giving information or directions: *We saw a notice of today's motion picture outside the theater.* **5** telling that one is leaving or must leave rented quarters or a job at a given time: *A month's notice is required from whichever person wishes to end this agreement.*
   1, 3–5 *noun,* **2,** *verb.*

a. _____ There is a **notice** in the store window that says "On Vacation."

b. _____ The chicken **noticed** each piece of corn on the ground.

c. _____ She gave only a week's **notice** before she left her apartment.

d. _____ Nobody **noticed** the hole in my shirt.

3. **pre mi um** (prē´mē əm), **1** reward; prize: *Some magazines give premiums for obtaining new subscriptions.* **2** money paid for insurance: *Father pays premiums on his life insurance four times a year.* **3** unusual or unfair value: *Our teacher puts a high premium on neatness and punctuality.*
   noun.

a. _____ We pay only one **premium** a year on our car insurance.

b. _____ The toys and candy are **premiums** given by the new store in our neighborhood.

c. _____ Why does she put such a **premium** on success?

d. _____ If I sell one hundred books, will you give me a **premium**?

4. **treat** (trēt), **1** act toward: *Father treats our new car with care.* **2** think of; consider; regard: *He treated his mistake as a joke.* **3** deal with to relieve or cure: *The dentist is treating my toothache.* **4** deal with; discuss: *This magazine treats the progress of medicine.* **5** express in literature or art: *The author treats the characters of his story so that you feel you know them.* **6** give food, drink, or amusement: *He treated his friends to a soda, and they treated him to a movie.* **7** gift of food, drink, or amusement: *"This is my treat,"* she said. **8** anything that gives pleasure: *Being in the country is a treat to her.*
   1–6 *verb,* **7, 8** *noun.*

a. _____ Some doctors **treat** more than twenty people each day.

b. _____ Our teacher **treats** each student fairly.

c. _____ Let me **treat** you to supper tonight.

d. _____ Going to a movie like this is a real **treat**!

CHECK ON PAGE 91

B. COMPOUND WORDS

> The parts of a family and many numbers larger than twelve may be **compound words**.
>
> Many of these words are written with a hyphen between the two or three parts of the compound word.
>
> He became a father at the age of twenty, a **grandfather** at the age of **forty-three**, and a **great-grandfather** at the age of **sixty-seven**.

Say each word and write it on the line next to the number. Then complete each sentence by adding one of the words at the left to the word below each blank, and writing the new compound word on the blank.

uncle 19. _____

sixty 20. _____

birth 21. _____

grandfather 22. _____

grandmother 23. _____

daughter 24. _____

aunt 25. _____

sister 26. _____

grandson 27. _____

Fifty 28. _____

brother 29. _____

second 30. _____

a. Your _____ Ned will be _____
           great-   -eight
next Monday.

b. Your _____ came to this country on his tenth
           great-
_____.
     day

c. She became a _____ when her
               great-
_____ had her first baby this morning.
  grand

d. Did you know that your _____ is also my
                       great-
mother's _____?
      -in-law

e. His _____ goes to school on
           great-
_____ Street.
  -first

f. His _____ just had his _____
      -in-law   fifty-
birthday.

CHECK ON PAGE 91

31

C. SENTENCE PATTERNS

> The sentences you read may be **active** or **passive**. In an **active sentence**, the subject does the action. In a **passive sentence**, something is done **to** the subject. The subject does **not** do the action.
>
> | | Subject | Verb | |
> |---|---|---|---|
> | Active: | The lion | **ate** | the man. (The lion does the action.) |
> | Passive: | The man | **was** eat**en by** | the lion. (The action was done to the man.) |
>
> There are three clues that show when a sentence is **passive**:
> (1) A form of the helping verb **be** is added before the verb.
> (2) A passive ending, often **d(ed)** or **n(en)**, is added to the verb.
> (3) The word **by** appears before the noun that is doing the action.

1. *Study the sentence pairs below. Draw a circle around the noun that does the action in each sentence. Draw a line under the other clues that show a passive sentence in the second sentence in each pair. The first one is done for you.*

    a. *Active:*   (Angela) drew that picture five minutes ago.

       Passive: That picture was drawn by (Angela) five minutes ago.

    b. *Active:*   The man hears a noise in the alley.

       Passive: A noise is heard in the alley by the man.

    c. *Active:*   My mother will buy the pen and pencil set.

       Passive: The pen and pencil set will be bought by my mother.

    d. *Active:*   The doctor read the notice in the papers.

       Passive: The notice in the papers was read by the doctor.

    e. *Active:*   Could anyone pay the premium on the insurance policy?

       Passive: Could the premium on the insurance policy be paid by anyone?

2. *Complete the sentence pairs below. If the finished sentence is **active**, write the rest of the **passive** sentence. If the finished sentence is **passive**, write the rest of the **active** sentence.*

    a. They made the report in secret.

       The report _____ by them.

    b. Each student _____.

       The lesson was repeated by each student.

c. The children had torn the old blanket into rags.

_____ by the children.

d. Did your father _____ ?

Was that book found inside the car by your father?

CHECK ON PAGE 91

D. SYLLABICATION

You have learned about two kinds of syllables. First, a closed syllable ends in a consonant sound, as in both syllables of the word **pic-nic**. The vowel sound in a closed syllable is usually short.

The second kind of syllable is an open syllable, which ends in a vowel. The first syllable is usually open when a single consonant follows the first vowel, as in the word **re-turn**. The vowel sound in an open syllable is usually long.

Divide each word into syllables and write the divided word on the first blank line. Then, on the second blank line, identify the first syllable as open or closed. The first one has been done for you.

1. manner   *man ner*   *closed*

2. blanket   _____   _____

3. secret   _____   _____

4. remain   _____   _____

5. angry   _____   _____

6. silent   _____   _____

7. except   _____   _____

CHECK ON PAGE 91

CA-23

A. WORDS IN SENTENCES

1. *Say each word and write it on the line next to the number. Then complete each sentence using the words you wrote.*

neck 1. _____

collar 2. _____

license 3. _____

curb 4. _____

judge 5. _____

bite 6. _____

wagged 7. _____

urge 8. _____

flag 9. _____

travel 10. _____

closet 11. _____

manage 12. _____

wag 13. _____

whether 14. _____

a. That shirt _____ was too small, so he wore a shirt with a crew _____.

b. He was speeding when he drove his car over the _____, so the _____ took away his driver's _____.

c. That little dog _____ his tail, so I didn't think he would _____.

d. The speaker said we should _____ our friends to show respect for our country's _____.

e. I _____ two or three times each month, so I keep a bag ready in the _____.

f. Her dog is so sick, I don't know _____ it can _____ to _____ its tail.

CHECK ON PAGE 92

DICTIONARY—ENTRIES

2. *Study the four dictionary entries. Write the number of the definition that shows how the word is used in each sentence.*

1. **bite** (bīt), **1** seize, cut into, or cut off with the teeth: *She bit the apple. That nervous boy bites his nails.* **2** a piece bitten off; mouthful: *Eat the whole apple, not just a bite.* **3** a light meal; snack: *Have a bite with me now or you'll get hungry later.* **4** wound with teeth, fangs, or a sting: *My dog never bites. A mosquito bit me.* **5** a wound made by biting or stinging: *The man soon recovered from the snake's bite.* **6** a sharp, smarting pain: *We felt the bite of the wind.* **7** cause a sharp, smart pain to: *His fingers are bitten by frost.* **8** take a tight hold of; grip: *The jaws of a vise bite the wood they hold.* **9** take a bait; be caught: *The fish are biting well today.* **1, 4, 7–9** *verb* **bit**, **bit ten** or **bit**, **bit ing**, **2, 3, 5, 6** *noun*.

a. _____ Some dogs will **bite** anything that makes a sudden move.

b. _____ I'm so full I couldn't eat another **bite**!

c. _____ We could feel the **bite** of the freezing rain on our faces.

d. _____ If we fish where the pond is quiet, we should get a **bite**.

2. **li cense** (lī´sns), **1** permission given by law to do something: *A license to drive an automobile is issued by the state.* **2** paper, card, or plate showing such permission: *The policeman asked the reckless driver for his license.* **3** permit by law: *A doctor is licensed to practice medicine.* **4** too much liberty of action; lack of proper control; abuse of freedom.
1, 2, 4 *noun*, **3** *verb*, **li censed, li cens ing.**

a. ____ Would you like to see my driver's **license**?

b. ____ It takes years to earn a **license** to heal the sick.

c. ____ Are you **licensed** to rent rooms in this building?

d. ____ Do you need a **license** to sell insurance?

3. **man age** (man´ij), **1** control; conduct; handle; direct: *A good rider manages his horse well. They hired a man to manage the business.* **2** succeed in doing something: *I shall manage to keep warm with this blanket.* **3** get along: *We managed on very little money.*
1–3 *verb*, **man aged, man ag ing.**

a. ____ I don't know how he **managed** to stay so cool during the battle.

b. ____ He **manages** the family business.

c. ____ Do you need someone to **manage** this office?

d. ____ When he lost his job, he didn't know how he would **manage**.

4. **shad ow** (shad´ō), **1** shade made by some person, animal, or thing. Sometimes a person's shadow is much longer than he is, and sometimes much shorter. **2** darkness; partial shade: *Don't turn on the light; we like to sit in the shadow.* **3** a little bit; small degree; slight suggestion: *There's not a shadow of a doubt about his guilt.* **4** ghost. **5** follow closely, usually secretly: *The detective shadowed the suspected burglar.*
1–4 *noun*, **5** *verb*.

a. ____ My job was to **shadow** the person wearing dark glasses.

b. ____ We should be able to live without the **shadow** of a fear.

c. ____ At noon, I have almost no **shadow**.

d. ____ I like to watch the **shadows** grow longer late in the afternoon.

CHECK ON PAGE 92

B. SYNONYMS AND ANTONYMS

When two words have meanings which are almost the same, we say they are **synonyms**.

You are not **allowed** to **leave**. You are not **permitted** to **go**.

In these sentences, **allowed** and **permitted** are synonyms, and **leave** and **go** are synonyms.

Words that have nearly opposite meanings are called **antonyms**.

Jane is **slender** now, but she was very **fat** two years ago.

In this sentence, **slender** and **fat** are antonyms.

CA-23

1. *Say each word and write it on the line next to the number. Then write a* **synonym** *for the word below the blank in each sentence. Each word will be used once.*

repair 15. _____

remain 16. _____

prepare 17. _____

reply 18. _____

smash 19. _____

leash 20. _____

a. Why would anyone want to _____ my car window?
   break

b. Please _____ in your seats; the fire has been put out.
   stay

c. Tie the _____ to the dog's collar before you take it out for a walk.
   rope

d. I could hear the reporter's question, but I couldn't hear the police officer's _____ to the question.
   answer

e. It will only take two hours to _____ your car.
   fix

f. The next act begins in three minutes, so we'd better _____.
   get ready

2. *Say each word and write it on the blank next to the number. Then write an* **antonym** *for the word below the blank in each sentence. Each word will be used once.*

clever 21. _____

wise 22. _____

shadow 23. _____

truth 24. _____

backward 25. _____

g. If you step out of the _____, I can take a better picture.
   light

h. They were supposed to walk _____ when they left the king's court.
   forward

i. I do not think it was _____ to tie the cans on that dog's tail.
   stupid

j. Who said that the _____ will make us free?
   lie

k. Many people believe that the oldest men and women are the most _____.
   silly.

CHECK ON PAGE 92

36

C. WORD FUNCTIONS

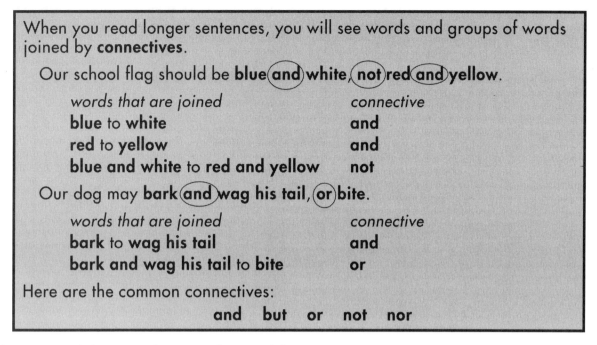

When you read longer sentences, you will see words and groups of words joined by **connectives**.

Our school flag should be **blue** (and) **white,** (not) **red** (and) **yellow.**

words that are joined	connective
blue to **white**	**and**
red to **yellow**	**and**
blue and white to **red and yellow**	**not**

Our dog may **bark** (and) **wag his tail,** (or) **bite.**

words that are joined	connective
bark to **wag his tail**	**and**
bark and wag his tail to **bite**	**or**

Here are the common connectives:

and   but   or   not   nor

Read the sentences below. First draw a circle around the connective. Then underline the word or word groups that are joined by this connective.

a. The children wanted to stay home, not travel.

b. He opened his shirt collar and rubbed his neck.

c. I opened the closet and took out my shirt.

d. I wondered whether to paint the desk or the chairs.

e. She had a bowl of soup and a glass of milk.

CHECK ON PAGE 92

D. SYLLABICATION

You know that in words having a single consonant after the first vowel, the vowel usually ends the first syllable, as in **e-ven**.

But there are many cases where such a word is divided after that consonant instead of after the first vowel, as in the word **cab-in**.

It is important that you say a word to see how to divide it into syllables. If the first vowel sound is long, you probably need an open syllable, so you divide the word after the vowel:

e-ven, si-lent, o-ver

If the first vowel sound is short, you probably need a closed syllable, so divide the word after the consonant.

cab-in, pris-on, vis-it

Divide each word into syllables and write the divided word on the blank line.

1. license   _____

2. travel   _____

3. river   _____

4. repeat   _____

5. dozen   _____

6. human   _____

7. notice   _____

8. rapid   _____

9. lemon   _____

10. prepare   _____

CHECK ON PAGE 92

A. WORDS IN SENTENCES

1. *Say each word and write it on the line next to the number. Then complete each sentence using the words you wrote.*

paddle   1. _____

canoe   2. _____

jacket   3. _____

cream   4. _____

knee   5. _____

couple   6. _____

red   7. _____

rise   8. _____

yellow   9. _____

shy   10. _____

stare   11. _____

a. Instead of saying "Mind your own business," he told me to "_____ my own _____."

b. She dropped her ice _____ all over my new _____.

c. She has a _____ of cuts on each _____.

d. The sun and moon usually look _____, but they seem _____ when they _____ and when they set.

e. He says he doesn't feel _____ unless people _____ at him.

CHECK ON PAGE 93

DICTIONARY—ENTRIES

2. *Study the four dictionary entries below. You can see that each word has more than one meaning. The meaning comes from the way each word is used in a sentence. Write the number of the definition in front of each sentence at the right of each entry.*

1. **cou ple** (kup´əl), **1** two things of the same kind that go together; pair: *He bought a couple of tires for his bicycle.* **2** people who are married, engaged, or partners in a dance. **3** join together: *The brakeman coupled the freight cars.* **1, 2,** *noun,* **3** *verb,* **cou pled, cou pling.**

a. ____ We must **couple** the last car to the train.

b. ____ I took a **couple** of my friends to the party.

c. ____ Bette and Ray make an attractive **couple**.

d. ____ I like those dresses so much, I'll buy a **couple**.

2. **cream** (krēm), **1** the oily, yellowish part of milk. Cream rises to the top when milk is allowed to stand. Butter is made from cream. **2** a fancy sweet dessert or candy made of cream: *chocolate creams.* **3** make a smooth mixture like cream: *She creamed butter and sugar together for a cake.* **4** an oily preparation put on the skin to make it smooth and soft. **5** yellowish white. **6** best part of anything: *The cream of a class is made up of the best students.* **1, 2, 4, 6** *noun,* **3** *verb,* **5** *adjective.*

a. ____ Add three eggs, then **cream** the cake batter.

b. ____ She bought hand **cream**.

c. ____ That shirt is not white; it's **cream** colored.

d. ____ The richest part of milk is called **cream**.

CA-24

3. **rise** (rīz), **1** get up from a lying, sitting, or kneeling position; stand up; get up: *Please rise from your seat when you recite.* **2** get up from sleep or rest: *The farmer's wife rises at 6 every morning.* **3** go up; come up: *The kite rises in the air. Bread rises. Mercury rises in a thermometer on a hot day. Fish rise to the surface.* **4** go higher; increase: *Butter rose five cents in price. The wind rose rapidly. His anger rose at that remark.* **5** going up; increase: *We watched the rise of the balloon. There has been a great rise in prices since the war.* **6** advance in importance or rank: *He rose from office clerk to president of the company.* **7** slope upward: *Hills rise in the distance.* **8** an upward slope: *The rise of the hill is gradual. The house is situated on a rise.*
1–4, 6, 7 *verb*, **rose, ris en, ris ing, 5, 8** *noun*.

a. _____ Coffee cake **rises** when you bake it.

b. _____ There has been a **rise** each week in the cost of most foods.

c. _____ Our cabin was built on the top of a small **rise**.

d. _____ They **rise** each morning at seven.

4. **shy** (shī), **1** uncomfortable in company; bashful: *He is shy and dislikes parties.* **2** easily frightened away; timid: *A deer is a shy animal.* **3** start back or aside suddenly: *The horse shied at the newspaper blowing along the ground.*
1, 2 *adjective*, **shy er, shy est,** or **shi er, shi est, 3** *verb*, **shied, shy ing.**

a. _____ She is too **shy** to meet many new people.

b. _____ The animal **shied** away when it saw my bright red shirt.

c. _____ Most wild animals are **shy** of humans.

d. _____ Come on, speak up! Don't be **shy**.

CHECK ON PAGE 93

B. WORD MEANINGS

The names of the twelve months of the year and the seven days of the week always begin with a capital letter.
The eighth month of the year is **August**; **November** is the eleventh.
The name **Sunday** comes from the sun, but **Monday** is named for the moon.
We use a capital letter because we are **naming** a particular month or a particular day.

Say each word and write it on the line next to the number. Then complete each sentence using the words you wrote.

September 12. _____

debt 13. _____

due 14. _____

Tuesday 15. _____

baggage 16. _____

Thursday 17. _____

polite 18. _____

a. Our _____ is _____ on _____, the first of _____.

b. They were very _____ but they said we could not get our _____ until _____ night or Friday morning.

40

collect 19. _____

interest 20. _____

February 21. _____

Saturday 22. _____

meant 23. _____

puzzle 24. _____

Wednesday 25. _____

October 26. _____

calm 27. _____

January 28. _____

payment 29. _____

December 30. _____

c. She will lend you the money now, but she won't _____ any _____ until next _____.

d. They won't know what the _____ really _____ until they see the answer in the paper next _____.

e. The weather will be fair and the sea will be _____ from _____ until the end of _____.

f. Can I make the _____ this year on _____ 31, or should I wait until the new year and pay you in _____?

CHECK ON PAGE 93

C. WORD FUNCTIONS

Words or groups of words may be joined by the **connectives and**, **or**, **but**, **not**, or **nor**. Sometimes **sentences** may be joined by words we call **conjunctions**. A conjunction may appear in the middle of a longer sentence, between what might have been two shorter sentences.

The leader was there, (and) the band played well.

A conjunction may appear in front of the first shorter sentence.

(When) the leader was there, the band played well.

A conjunction may also appear in the middle of a longer sentence when one shorter sentence appears inside another.

The band, (while) the leader was there, played as well as they could.

Here are some words you know that are used as conjunctions:

after	however	rather than	though
although	if	since	unless
and	in fact	so	until
because	in other words	so that	when
before	instead	such as	whenever
but	meanwhile	that is	whether
even	nevertheless	then	while
except	or	therefore	yet

41

CA-24

Study the pairs of short sentences below. Choose the conjunction that can join them to make one longer sentence. Then write the longer sentence on the lines. If the conjunction starts with a capital letter, use it to start the new sentence. If not, start the new sentence with the word in the shorter sentence that starts with a capital letter.

a. they found his baggage,
   he became calm again.
   Before   After

   _____

   _____

b. She dropped her eyes
   she was shy
   although   because

   _____

   _____

c. Today is Tuesday
   we must make the first payment on our debt.
   so   although

   _____

   _____

d. The flag was red at the top
   there was some yellow at the bottom.
   or   and

   _____

   _____

e. the canoe turned over,
   we lost our paddle.
   When   Instead

   _____

   _____

CHECK ON PAGE 93

D. SYLLABICATION/PRONUNCIATION GUIDE

When a word that ends in *le* has a consonant before the *le*, you divide it so that the consonant begins the last syllable, as in the following examples:

fa-**ble**, gam-**ble**, nee-**dle**

Divide each word into syllables and write the divided word on the blank line.

1. paddle   _____

2. simple   _____

3. trouble   _____

4. middle   _____

5. battle   _____

6. scramble   _____

7. straddle   _____

8. rattle   _____

9. table   _____

10. couple   _____

CHECK ON PAGE 93

CA-25

A. WORDS IN SENTENCES

1. *Say each word and write it on the line next to the number. Then complete each sentence using the words you wrote.*

replace   1. _____

handle   2. _____

barrel   3. _____

     spy   4. _____

citizen   5. _____

    zone   6. _____

inches   7. _____

discharge   8. _____

illness   9. _____

arrest 10. _____

criminal 11. _____

a. You can't lift that _____ until you _____ the broken _____.

b. She looked like any other _____ of that country, but she was acting as a _____ for the enemy.

c. Their car was parked a few _____ inside the loading _____, so they got a ticket.

d. We will _____ him from the hospital now that his _____ has been treated.

e. Every _____ must be told of his or her rights by the person who makes an _____.

CHECK ON PAGE 94

DICTIONARY—ENTRIES

2. *Study the four dictionary entries below. Each word has more than one meaning. The meanings are numbered. Write the number that shows which meaning is used in each sentence to the right of the entry.*

1. **ar rest** (ə rest´), **1** seize by authority of the law; take to jail or court: *A police officer arrested the thief.* **2** a stopping; seizing: *We saw the arrest of the burglar.* **3** stop; check: *Filling a tooth arrests decay.* **4** catch and hold: *Our attention was arrested by the sound of a shot.* **1, 3, 4** *verb,* **2** *noun.*

a. ____ The anchor will **arrest** the movement of the ship.

b. ____ If your driving is too dangerous, you may be **arrested**.

c. ____ They didn't notice the signs of a struggle, but the blood on the floor **arrested** their attention.

d. ____ Freeze! You're under **arrest**!

2. **dis charge** (dis chärj´),   **1** unload (cargo or passengers) from ship, train, bus, or airplane: *The ship discharged its passengers at the dock.*   **2** unloading: *The discharge of this cargo will not take long.*   **3** fire off; shoot: *The policeman discharged his gun at the fleeing robbers.*   **4** firing off a gun or a blast: *The discharge of dynamite could be heard for three miles.*   **5** release; let go; dismiss; *to discharge a patient from a hospital, to discharge a servant.*   **6** release; letting go; dismissing: *The prisoner expects his discharge from jail next week.*   **7** perform (a duty): *He discharged all the errands he had been given.*   **8** performing of a duty: *A public official should be honest in the discharge of his duties.*
1, **3**, **5**, **7** *verb*, **dis charged**, **dis charg ing**, **2**, **4**, **6**, **8** *noun*.

a. _____   He **discharged** all the duties of his office.

b. _____   She may be **discharged** from the hospital tomorrow.

c. _____   They were told to expect their **discharge** from the service.

d. _____   Be careful! He has only **discharged** five bullets from that gun.

3. **han dle** (han´dl),   **1** part of a thing made to be held or grasped by the hand. Spoons, pitchers, hammers, and pails have handles.   **2** touch, feel, or use with the hand: *Don't handle that book until you wash your hands.*   **3** manage; direct: *The captain handles his soldiers well.*   **4** behave or act when handled: *This car handles easily.*   **5** treat: *The thoughtless boy handled his cat roughly.*   **6** deal in; trade in: *That store handles meat and groceries.*
1 *noun*, **2–6** *verb*, **han dled**, **han dling**.

a. _____   The police **handled** the angry crowd easily.

b. _____   This store does not **handle** women's clothes.

c. _____   The **handle** of that bucket is broken.

d. _____   Does your small car **handle** better than my large one?

4. **re place** (ri plās´),   **1** fill or take the place of: *He replaced his brother as captain.*   **2** get another in place of: *I will replace the cup I broke.*   **3** put back; put in place again: *Replace the books on the shelves.*
1–3 *verb*, **re placed**, **re plac ing**.

a. _____   Please **replace** each book when you have finished reading it.

b. _____   She has been sent to **replace** Captain Williams.

c. _____   He says he will **replace** each dish that he breaks.

d. _____   These new stop signs will **replace** the old ones.

CHECK ON PAGE 94

B. PREFIXES

When the prefix **un** appears before a word, it adds the meaning "not" to the word.

Your car is **un**safe at any speed!
↑not safe

When the letter **a** appears before a word, it makes a completely new word. The meaning of the new word may or may not be related to the meaning of the original word.

Our car went **a**head in the race.
↑ **a head** is not related to **ahead**

Say each word and write it on the line next to the number. Then complete each sentence using two of the three words you wrote.

disturbed 12. _____

undisturbed 13. _____

President 14. _____

a.   Be sure that the _____ is not

_____ while he is writing his letters.

45

apply 15. _____

employed 16. _____

unemployed 17. _____

adrift 18. _____

astray 19. _____

dangerous 20. _____

theater 21. _____

able 22. _____

unable 23. _____

easy 24. _____

uneasy 25. _____

height 26. _____

fought 27. _____

ashamed 28. _____

unashamed 29. _____

b. Since he was _____, he wanted to _____ for as many jobs as he could.

c. We knew it was _____ to be _____ without a motor in a busy seaport.

d. I was _____ to get tickets for the _____ today, but we can go tomorrow, if you'd like.

e. Looking down from such a great _____ made us all feel _____, but only Tony was afraid.

f. We made him feel _____ because he _____ so often.

CHECK ON PAGE 94

C. SENTENCE PATTERNS

1. In a sentence or a paragraph, words known as **pronouns** can **take the place of nouns**. The **personal pronouns** take the place of words that name persons, places, or things. The pronoun **it** can also take the place of whole phrases, sentences, or ideas.

I	you	she	he	it	we	they
I	you	she	he	it	we	they
me	you	her	him	it	us	them
my	your	her	his	its	our	their
mine	yours	hers	his	its	ours	theirs

When you see a **pronoun**, you need to remember what person, place, or thing is being talked about.

Four people ran for **the job of class president**. **Sal** and **Tommy** got eight votes between **them**. Ray got ten votes, and **Susannah** won with fourteen. **It** will not be a difficult job for **her**.

pronoun	refers to
them	*Sal* and *Tommy*
it	*her job of class president*

Which person does the pronoun **her** refer to?

Read each group of sentences below. Decide which word or words the pronouns in dark print refer to. Then write the persons, places, or things that the pronoun refers to on the line at the right.

a. My father was discharged from the hospital.

   He said **he** never felt better.   He = _____

b. Looking for a new job is not easy.

   It can take a long time.   It = _____

c. Lift the barrel by that handle.

   It is heavy, so be careful!   It = _____

d. During **her** illness, Gwen lost five pounds.   her = _____

   She looked very pale.   She = _____

e. The citizens would not listen to the spy.   They = _____

   They told **him** to go back to **his** own country.   him = _____

   his = _____

2.
> Another type of pronoun, a **relative pronoun**, appears in longer sentences. **Who**, **which**, and **that** refer to a noun that has already appeared in the sentence.
>
>   This is the **boy who** chased the **car that** hit the puppy.
>
> **Who** refers to nouns, like **boy**, that name persons. **That** or **which** refer to nouns, like **car**, that name places or things.

Read the longer sentences below. Find the relative pronoun in each sentence. Draw an arrow from the pronoun to the noun that the pronoun refers to.

a. The officer who made the arrest was discharged from the hospital.

b. The doctors found a cure for the illness that took so many lives.

c. The truck that I'm looking for is painted red and yellow.

d. After his arrest, the man who had robbed so many citizens broke down and cried.

e. This is the theater in which President Lincoln was shot.

f. He now has the horse which used to be John's.

CHECK ON PAGE 94

D. SYLLABICATION

A syllable that is added to the beginning of a word to change its meaning is called a **prefix**. The word the prefix is added to is called the **root word**.

un (prefix) + **safe** (root word) = **unsafe**

When you add the prefix **un** to a word, it means **not**. Look at the following examples:

un safe — **not** safe
un clean — **not** clean
un happy — **not** happy

Adding the prefix **dis** often makes the meaning of the word the opposite of what it was before, as in these examples:

| like | **not** like | **dis**like |
| please | **not** please | **dis**please |

Since both **un** and **dis** can have the meaning **not**, you must be careful to use the correct prefix for the root word. If you have doubts, use a dictionary to help you.

The prefix **re** often means doing **again**. Look at the following examples:

rename — **name again**
repaint — **paint again**

*Add **un**, **re**, or **dis** to make words that belong in the sentences.*

1. The boy was _____happy because he lost his dog.

2. You'd better _____read the story you read yesterday.

3. I can never _____pay you for all that you have done.

4. She was _____willing to give us the money we needed.

5. His boss was so _____pleased with his work that she fired him.

6. He soon began looking for a job because he didn't like being _____employed.

7. The room was in _____order after the party.

8. When he went to jail, he brought _____honor to his family.

9. I'm sorry that I am _____able to help you.

10. They _____built their house after it had burned down.

CHECK ON PAGE 94

REVIEW 21–25

Say each word and write it on the line next to the number. Then complete each part by writing one word on each blank line. The numbers under the lines tell you which words to choose from.

A.

1. _____ knee
2. _____ alcohol
3. _____ growl
4. _____ handle
5. _____ unemployed
6. _____ wise
7. _____ daughter
8. _____ citizen
9. _____ fumes
10. _____ private
11. _____ relax
12. _____ refuse
13. _____ policy
14. _____ truth
15. _____ unsafe
16. _____ unable

My name is Jennie, and I have a problem with _____ (1 or 2). I'd like to tell you my story. I didn't always drink. It started when I lost my job. I couldn't _____ (3 or 4) being _____ (5 or 6). At that time, I'd drink only when in the company of friends. But after my _____ (7 or 8) took sick and almost died, I began drinking in _____ (9 or 10). I told myself that I was drinking to _____ (11 or 12). The _____ (13 or 14) is that I was _____ (15 or 16) to deal with my troubles and just wanted to escape life.

B.

17. _____ manage
18. _____ replace
19. _____ debt
20. _____ secret
21. _____ became
22. _____ spied
23. _____ clever
24. _____ yellow
25. _____ notice
26. _____ prepare
27. _____ paddled
28. _____ fought
29. _____ canoe
30. _____ theater
31. _____ silly
32. _____ shy
33. _____ wag
34. _____ stare
35. _____ polite
36. _____ red
37. _____ remain
38. _____ rise
39. _____ puzzled
40. _____ meant
41. _____ reply
42. _____ shock
43. _____ uncle
44. _____ silence

49

At first, I could _____ keeping my drinking a _____ . I _____
(17 or 18)   (19 or 20)   (21 or 22)

very _____ at hiding my problem. But before long, my family started to _____
(23 or 24)   (25 or 26)

that I was changing. I _____ with my husband all the time. One day my daughter came home
(27 or 28)

from school to find me passed out on the kitchen table.

Another time I had too many drinks before going to the _____ with my family. I soon
(29 or 30)

began acting _____ and talking out loud in the middle of the show. Everyone began to
(31 or 32)

_____ at me. The manager was _____ , but he told us we couldn't
(33 or 34)   (35 or 36)

_____ .
(37 or 38)

When we got outside, my daughter asked, "Why must you drink?" She had tears in her eyes.

I felt terrible. I had never _____ to hurt her. But my only _____ to her
(39 or 40)   (41 or 42)

question was _____ . How could she understand when I didn't understand it myself?
(43 or 44)

C.

45. _____   46. _____   59. _____   60. _____
         Friday   curb   payment   due

47. _____   48. _____   61. _____   62. _____
          zone   January   students   baggage

49. _____   50. _____   63. _____   64. _____
          blaze   travel   insurance   interest

51. _____   52. _____   65. _____   66. _____
          dozen   premium   rag   blanket

53. _____   54. _____   67. _____   68. _____
         closet   barrel   calm   stupid

55. _____   56. _____   69. _____   70. _____
         collect   bite   dangerous   grand

57. _____   58. _____   71. _____   72. _____
         pencil   jacket   smashed   wagged

The turning point for me came one snowy _____ in _____ . The day before, my
(45 or 46)   (47 or 48)

husband had to _____ out of town on business. My daughter was at a school dance, and I was
(49 or 50)

home alone. I had finished off a _____ drinks by the time I received a call from my daughter.
(51 or 52)

"I'm not feeling well. Can you pick me up?" she said.

"Sure," I replied. I went to the _____ to _____ my _____, hat,
(53 or 54)   (55 or 56)   (57 or 58)

and gloves. But I had trouble putting them on _____ to the state I was in.
(59 or 60)

Drunk as I was, it was a wonder I made it to the school at all. Once inside, I received cold stares from

some of the _____, but they were of no _____ to me. I found my daughter and we left.
(61 or 62)   (63 or 64)

By that time, a _____ of snow already covered the road. It was _____ of me
(65 or 66)   (67 or 68)

to drive. A drunk driver is _____ even in good weather. Suddenly, my daughter yelled "Stop!"
(69 or 70)

But it was too late. Going right through a stop sign, I _____ into another car.
(71 or 72)

D.

73. _____   74. _____   83. _____   84. _____
         cream   arrest   collared   urged

75. _____   76. _____   85. _____   86. _____
        criminal   president   neck   whether

77. _____   78. _____   87. _____   88. _____
         inches   court   silent   lonely

79. _____   80. _____   89. _____   90. _____
         judge   aunt   become   shadowed

81. _____   82. _____   91. _____   92. _____
        license   leash   repeat   repair

No one was badly hurt, but I could have killed someone—maybe even my own daughter. I found myself

under _____, and knew what it felt like to be a _____. In _____, the
(73 or 74)   (75 or 76)   (77 or 78)

_____ threw the book at me. He took away my _____ and ordered me to pay a
(79 or 80)   (81 or 82)

heavy fine. He didn't send me to jail, but warned he would if there were a next time. Then he

_____ me to get help. By this time, even I had to admit that I had a problem,
(83 or 84)

_____ I wanted to or not.
(85 or 86)

My husband and daughter were _____ in the court, but had plenty to say when we got home.
(87 or 88)

They were tough on me, but no tougher than I was on myself. I didn't like what I had _____. I
(89 or 90)

told them I'd get help and try to _____ some of the damage I had done to my family.
(91 or 92)

E.

93. _____
human

94. _____
foreman

99. _____
illness

100. _____
alley

95. _____
thirsty

96. _____
height

101. _____
flag

102. _____
treat

97. _____
pen

98. _____
couple

103. _____
discharge

104. _____
apply

Now, I haven't had a drink in ten months, and I feel great. Sure, I'm _____; I still find
                                                                    (93 or 94)

myself _____ for alcohol at times. I'd like to have a _____ of drinks, but I won't.
        (95 or 96)   (97 or 98)

I've taken control of my life.

Some say drinking is an _____. Maybe it is, but a doctor can't make you better; you have to
                         (99 or 100)

_____ yourself. You do this by taking things one day at a time. If you really _____
(101 or 102)   (103 or 104)

yourself, you can beat this thing. I did.

CHECK ON PAGE 95

A. WORDS IN SENTENCES

1. *Say each word and write it on the line next to the number. Then complete each sentence using the words you wrote.*

college 1. _____

chief 2. _____

carrier 3. _____

teammate 4. _____

aim 5. _____

flat 6. _____

fourth 7. _____

prediction 8. _____

coach 9. _____

themselves 10. _____

ought 11. _____

peaceful 12. _____

mate 13. _____

predict 14. _____

imagine 15. _____

imagination 16. _____

a. He was the _____ ball-_____ on our _____ football team.

b. My _____ was good, but my _____ was knocked _____ on the ground and couldn't catch the ball.

c. On the _____ down, the _____ made a _____ that we would win.

d. People who think all nations _____ to live in peace should be more _____ _____.

e. How can you _____ the name of the person who will be your _____?

f. I can't _____ how you came to have such a good _____.

CHECK ON PAGE 96

DICTIONARY—ENTRIES

2. *Read each dictionary entry below. The meaning of each word depends on the way it is used in a sentence. Write the number of the meaning in front of the sentence at the right that uses this meaning.*

1. **aim** (ām), **1** point or direct (a gun or a blow) in order to hit: *He aimed at the can but missed.* **2** act of pointing or directing at something: *His aim was so poor that he missed the can.* **3** direct words or acts so as to influence a certain person or action: *The coach's talk was aimed at the boys who had not played fair.* **4** try: *She aimed to please her teachers.* **5** purpose: *Her aim was to do two years' work in one.*
1, **3**, **4** *verb*, **2**, **5** *noun*.

a. ____ He has only one **aim** in life: to be successful.

b. ____ The wind spoiled his **aim** and blew the arrow aside.

c. ____ **Aim** the gun a little below the center.

d. ____ She **aimed** her brightest smile at the TV camera.

53

2. **chief** (chēf), **1** head of a tribe or group; leader; person highest in rank or authority: *A fire chief is the head of a group of fire fighters.* **2** at the head; leading: *the chief engineer of a building project.* **3** most important; main: *The chief thing in school is your work.* **1** *noun*, **2, 3** *adjective*.

a. _____ The Indian **chief** was the leader of all the people in the tribe.

b. _____ In the north, the **chief** river is called Bear Brook.

c. _____ My mother is the **chief** person on the rescue team.

d. _____ In that company, his **chief** job is getting along with the workers.

3. **coach** (kōch), **1** a large, old-fashioned, closed carriage with seats inside. Those which carried passengers along a regular run, with stops for meals and fresh horses, often had seats on top too. **2** a passenger car of a railroad train. **3** bus. **4** a class of passenger accommodations on a commercial aircraft at lower rates than first class. **5** person who teaches or trains athletic teams: *a football coach.* **6** train or teach: *He coaches the football team.* **1–5** *noun, plural* **coaches**, **6** *verb*.

a. _____ The **coach** stopped every twenty miles to get fresh horses.

b. _____ When she travels on business, she never flies **coach**.

c. _____ She teaches music and **coaches** the basketball team.

d. _____ The baseball **coach** is my brother.

4. **flat** (flat), **1** smooth and level; even: *flat land.* **2** horizontal; at full length: *The storm left the trees flat on the ground.* **3** the flat part: *with the flat of the sword.* **4** not very deep or thick: *A plate is flat.* **5** with little air in it: *A nail or sharp stone can cause a flat tire.* **6** tire with little air in it. **7** positive; not to be changed: *A flat refusal is complete.* **8** without much life, interest, or flavor; dull: *a flat voice. Plain food tastes flat.* **9** below the true pitch in music: *sing flat.* **10** tone one-half step below natural pitch: *music written in B flat.* **11** make flat; become flat. **1, 2, 4, 5, 7, 8** *adjective*, **flat ter, flat test, 3, 6, 10** *noun*, **9** *adverb*, **11** *verb*, **flat ted, flat ting**.

a. _____ The last note she sang was a little **flat**.

b. _____ It took twenty minutes to change the **flat**.

c. _____ After ten minutes, the drink tasted **flat**.

d. _____ The officer knocked the criminals **flat** on their backs.

CHECK ON PAGE 96

B. SUFFIXES

The ending **ship** adds the meaning "a way of being" to a noun.
I have a lot of **friends** because I believe in **friendship**.
Friendship is the way of being a friend.

The ending **al** adds the meaning "having to do with" to a noun. Sometimes the spelling and pronunciation of the noun is changed when this ending is added.
When he takes **office** in January, his first **official** act will be to say "Thank you."

Say each word and write it on the line next to the number. Then complete each sentence using the words you wrote.

hard 17. _____

hardship 18. _____

citizen 19. _____

citizenship 20. _____

penman 21. _____

penmanship 22. _____

crime 23. _____

criminal 24. _____

nation 25. _____

national 26. _____

addition 27. _____

additional 28. _____

a. It is _____ to be happy in a time of great _____.

b. Each _____ should study the meaning of the word _____.

c. He is a poor _____, but _____ was never that important to him.

d. Some police chiefs feel that allowing a known _____ to be free on the streets is a _____.

e. Will their _____ work together in a time of _____ trouble?

f. Building an _____ room onto your house will not be hard, but each _____ you make will cost money.

CHECK ON PAGE 96

C. SENTENCE PATTERNS

A sentence expresses at least one complete thought.

My coach used to love this college.

sentence 1

He played football here.

sentence 2

Two complete sentences, expressing two complete thoughts, are often combined by conjunctions.

My coach, (when) he played football here, used to love this college.

sentence 1 *sentence 2* *sentence 1*

The conjunction **when** shows that the action in both shorter sentences took place at the same time.

Here are some more words that are used to show time:

after	meanwhile	when
as	then	whenever
before	until	while

CA-26

Read the longer sentences below. Circle each conjunction. Then check the box to show whether the action in the shorter sentence, marked 2, takes place before, at the same time, or after the action in the sentence marked 1.

	before	at the same time	after
1.			
2.			
3.			
4.			
5.			

1. My mouth begins to water whenever

   1

   I see a piece of cake.

   2

2. I will write to you every week

   1

   until you come home again.

   2

3. Just as I got to the bus stop,

   1

   I saw the bus pull away.

   2

4. The boss read the sales report; meanwhile,

   1

   the salesman started looking for a new job.

   2

5. While I was sleeping,

   1

   someone was breaking into my house.

   2

CHECK ON PAGE 96

D. SYLLABICATION

You have already seen how you can change the meaning of a root word by adding a prefix. You can also change the meaning by adding an **ending** to the root word called a **suffix**.

help (root word) + **ful** (suffix) = **helpful**

The suffix **ful** can add the meaning **full of** to the root word, as with the following words:

help**ful**, beauti**ful**, cheer**ful**

The suffix **ful** can also mean **as much as something can hold**, as with these words:

pocket**ful**, cup**ful**, hand**ful**

The suffix **less** usually adds the meaning **without**, as with these examples:

use**less** — **without** use
home**less** — **without** a home
friend**less** — **without** friends

Three other common suffixes are **ness** (the state of being), **ly** (in a way) and **able** (that can be). Look at the following examples:

dark**ness** — **the state of being dark**
bad**ly** — **in a bad way**
enjoy**able** — **that can be enjoyed**

Use the root word below the line and a suffix from the box to make a word that belongs in each sentence.

| ful | less | ness | ly | able |

1. We had a very _____ vacation in the country.
   peace

2. When Martin was out of work, things looked _____ for his family.
   hope

3. Your handwriting isn't _____.
   read

4. Parents teach their children to be _____ when crossing the street.
   care

5. Not wanting to wake anyone, she came up the stairs very _____.
   quiet

6. I was pleased by the _____ of the children.
   polite

7. The cars rode _____ when they went by the school.
   slow

8. Maria was very tired after spending a _____ night.
   sleep

9. The doctor said that my problem was _____.
   treat

10. The boy was pleased by his own _____.
    clever

A. WORDS IN SENTENCES

1. *Say each word and write it on the line next to the number. Then complete each sentence using the words you wrote.*

sex   1. _____

pleasant   2. _____

pulse   3. _____

temperature   4. _____

cough   5. _____

skin   6. _____

infection   7. _____

medicine   8. _____

cure   9. _____

prevent   10. _____

dream   11. _____

appeared   12. _____

dinner   13. _____

comfortable   14. _____

bath   15. _____

potato   16. _____

fat   17. _____

gravy   18. _____

a. In a _____ manner, the nurse asked for my name, age, and _____.

b. I opened my mouth and he took my _____, then he put his hand on the inside of my arm to take my _____.

c. "Your _____ does feel warm," he told me, "and you do have a bad _____, but the doctor will fix you up in no time."

d. The doctor gave me some _____ to clear up my _____.

e. "I wish I could _____ illness," she said, "rather than trying to find a _____."

f. My doctor _____ that night in a _____.

g. She said, "Take a warm _____ after _____ and you will feel much more _____ at night."

h. The ad said, "You can eat a _____ without any _____ and you won't get _____."

CHECK ON PAGE 97

DICTIONARY—ENTRIES

2. *Read each dictionary entry below. The meaning of each word depends on the way it is used in a sentence. Write the number of the meaning in front of the sentence at the right that uses this meaning.*

1. **ap pear** (ə pir´), **1** be seen; come in sight: *One by one the stars appear.* **2** seem; look: *The apple appeared sound on the outside, but it was rotten inside.* **3** be published: *His latest book appeared more than a year ago.* **4** show or present oneself in public: *The singer will appear on the television program today.*
verb.

a. _____ Why does the sun **appear** to be larger when it sets?

b. _____ Her latest hit record **appeared** less than a week ago.

c. _____ In the evening the fires of the enemy camp **appear** in the distance.

d. _____ The president will not **appear** as expected.

2. **cough** (kôf), **1** force air from the lungs with sudden effort and noise. **2** act of coughing. **3** sound of coughing. **4** condition that causes repeated coughing: *Her cold had caused a bad cough.*
1 *verb,* **2-4** *noun.*

a. _____ If that **cough** gets worse, you should see a doctor.

b. _____ His **cough** shook his whole body.

c. _____ He **coughed** for a long time after he left the burning building.

d. _____ The theater was quiet except for the **coughing** of the people in the back seats.

3. **dream** (drēm), **1** something thought, felt, or seen during sleep: *I had a bad dream last night.* **2** something unreal like a dream; daydream: *The boy had dreams of being a hero.* **3** think, feel, hear, or see during sleep; have dreams: *The little boy dreamed that he was flying.* **4** think of (something) as possible; imagine: *The day was so bright that we never dreamed it would rain.*
1, 2 *noun,* **3, 4** *verb,* **dreamed** or **dreamt, dream ing.**

a. _____ Do you remember when Dr. King said, "I have a **dream**?"

b. _____ He **dreamed** of having a talk show on TV.

c. _____ It was only a **dream**, but I woke up really afraid.

d. _____ Did you know your eyes move when you **dream**?

4. **pulse** (puls), **1** the beating of the heart; the changing flow of blood in the arteries caused by the beating of the heart. **2** any regular, measured beat: *the pulse of an engine.* **3** beat; throb; vibrate: *His heart pulsed with joy.* **4** feeling; sentiment: *The pulse of the nation.*
1, 2, 4 *noun,* **3** *verb,* **pulsed, puls ing.**

a. _____ Her **pulse** is steady now; she'll be all right.

b. _____ He puts his finger on the **pulse** of the city when he writes his stories for the newspaper.

c. _____ The **pulse** of the music took everything else out of my mind.

d. _____ Her heart **pulsed** with happiness when she met the President.

CHECK ON PAGE 97

B. SUFFIXES

The suffix *th* is used in two ways:

(1) At the end of a number, *th* tells the position a thing has in a series of numbers.

There were ten games that afternoon and she won the **seventh** and the **ninth**.

Some numbers, like **six** and **seven**, are unchanged when *th* is added. Others, like **nine**, drop the final *e* before adding *th*. Still others change their spelling or their pronunciation:

five becomes **fifth**   **twenty** becomes **twentieth**

(2) The suffix *th* is also added to the end of words to make naming words. Both the spelling and pronunciation may change when the *th* is added.

It was a **long** race. They ran the **length** of the track seven times before the race was over.

Say each word and write it on the line next to the number. Then complete each sentence using one of the words you wrote.

heal 19. _____

health 20. _____

a. She nursed her puppy back to _____.

sixty 21. _____

sixtieth 22. _____

b. We had a big party for my grandfather when he was _____ years old.

nine 23. _____

ninth 24. _____

c. This is the _____ time I've called you to dinner!

five 25. _____

fifth 26. _____

d. Ellen was the _____ person in line.

wide 27. _____

width 28. _____

e. The _____ tells how far across something is.

deep 29. _____

depth 30. _____

f. No one knows the _____ of this ocean.

CHECK ON PAGE 97

C. SENTENCE PATTERNS

Two complete sentences, expressing two complete thoughts, are often joined by a **conjunction**. Sometimes the thought in the second sentence **explains** the first sentence by **giving an example** or by **saying the same thing in a different way**.

That piece of furniture is a daybed; **that is**, it folds out at night.

Here are the conjunctions you already know that are used **to explain**:

for example   in other words   such as   that is

Sometimes the thought in the second sentence is simply **added on** to the first.

That car was a good buy, **and** it looks good **too**.

Here are the conjunctions you already know that **add** new ideas:

and   also   furthermore   or   too

Read the sentences numbered 1 below. Circle each conjunction. Then check the box to show whether the idea in the sentence numbered 2 adds a new idea or explains the idea in the first sentence.

	explains	adds on
a. The coach was helping our team; in other words, 1 the team was getting much better. 2		
b. This suit appears to be comfortable; also, 1 it feels good. 2		
c. This dinner took too long to prepare; furthermore, 1 I dislike cold potatoes and gravy. 2		
d. Does your throat hurt, or have you started to cough in 1 2 the morning?		
e. Many people teach at City College; for example, 1 the coach teaches his team. 2		
f. John always meets me with a "smart" remark such as, 1 "How's by you?" 2		

D. SYLLABICATION/PRONUNCIATION GUIDE

After a word has been divided into syllables, you can use clues in each syllable to unlock the word. Look at this example:

sup-pose   The word is divided into two syllables between the middle consonants.

sup   The fact that the first syllable is closed is a clue that the **u** is short.

pose   The final **e** in the second syllable is a clue that the **e** is silent and the other vowel, **o**, is long.

You can also unlock longer words by dividing them into syllables. Look at the following example:

im-por-tant   The word is divided into three syllables between consonants.

im   The first syllable is closed, so the **i** probably has a short vowel sound.

por   In the second syllable, **o** followed by **r** has the sound of the little word **or**.

tant   The third syllable is closed, so the **a** probably has a short sound.

Divide each word into syllables and write the divided word on the blank line. Then circle the word that correctly completes each statement.

1. mutter   _____
   a. The **u** will be: long   short
   b. The **er** will make the same sound you hear in: car   after

2. reflex   _____
   a. The first **e** will be: long   short
   b. The second **e** will be: long   short

3. punish   _____
   a. The **u** will be: long   short
   b. The **sh** will make the same sound you hear in: wash   catch

4. entertain   _____
   a. The first **e** will be: long   short
   b. The **a** will be: long   short

5. romantic   _____
   a. The **o** will be: long   short
   b. The **a** and **i** will be: long   short
   c. The **c** will make the same sound you hear at the end of: face   picnic

CHECK ON PAGE 97

A. WORDS IN SENTENCES

1. *Say each word and write it on the line next to the number. Then complete each sentence using the words you wrote.*

butter   1. _____

bit   2. _____

brick   3. _____

cheese   4. _____

wagon   5. _____

cow   6. _____

guide   7. _____

prayer   8. _____

western   9. _____

vegetables   10. _____

ripe   11. _____

snake   12. _____

difficult   13. _____

swallow   14. _____

mayor   15. _____

decide   16. _____

excites   17. _____

excitement   18. _____

a. I'd like a little _____ of _____ on my bread.

b. He cut us a piece of _____ that was shaped like a big yellow _____.

c. Our _____ was put to work pulling the _____.

d. The _____ turned to the _____ sky and began to sing a long _____.

e. We had to throw out those _____ because they were too _____.

f. It is not _____ for a _____ to _____ an animal that is bigger than it is!

g. We couldn't _____ which person would make the best _____ of our town.

h. It may be true that voting _____ you, but in your _____, you should not have voted six times!

CHECK ON PAGE 98

2. *Read the four dictionary entries below. Match the definitions with one of the sentences at the right of the entry word by writing on the blank the number of the definition which shows how the word was used in the sentence.*

1. **brick** (brik), **1** block of clay baked by sun or fire. Bricks are used to build walls or houses and pave walks. **2** bricks: *Chimneys are usually built of brick.* **3** anything shaped like a brick: *Ice cream is often sold in bricks.* **4** build or pave with bricks; cover or fill in with bricks: *brick a walk, brick up an old window.*
1–3 *noun,* **4** *verb.*

a. _____ The walls of his house are built of special handmade **bricks**.

b. _____ We **bricked** up the door to our basement.

c. _____ The floor of the court is made of **brick**.

d. _____ When I took the cornbread out of the pan, it looked like a **brick**.

2. **guide** (gīd), **1** show the way; lead; direct: *The Indian scout guided the explorers through the mountain pass.* **2** person or thing that shows the way: *Tourists and hunters sometimes hire guides. The amount of money you have is a guide to how much you can spend.* **3** guidebook.
1 *verb,* **guid ed, guid ing; 2, 3** *noun.*

a. _____ Who will **guide** us through the desert?

b. _____ My father hired a **guide** to help him catch more fish.

c. _____ We bought a **guide** to the best vacation spots in America for only two dollars.

d. _____ The way you dress is a **guide** to what you want from life.

3. **prayer** (prer *or* prar), **1** act of praying. **2** thing prayed for: *Our prayers were granted.* **3** form of words to be used in praying: *the Lord's Prayer.* **4** form of worship. **5** an earnest request.
noun.

a. _____ She got down on her knees in **prayer**.

b. _____ The captain sent a **prayer** to the king to give him an easy death.

c. _____ This morning, my mother's **prayers** were answered.

d. _____ In Mel's church, there is a service called Morning **Prayer**.

4. **swal low** (swol´ō), **1** take into the stomach through the throat: *We swallow all our food and drink.* **2** take in; absorb: *The waves swallowed up the swimmer.* **3** believe too easily; accept without question or suspicion: *He will swallow any story.* **4** put up with; take meekly; accept without opposing or resisting: *He swallowed the insults of the bully without saying anything.* **5** keep back; keep from expressing: *She swallowed her displeasure and smiled.* **6** swallowing: *He took the bitter medicine at one swallow.* **7** amount swallowed at one time: *There are only about four swallows of water left in the bottle.*
1-5 *verb,* **6, 7** *noun.*

a. _____ She **swallowed** the pills instead of chewing them.

b. _____ He's so dumb, he'll **swallow** anything!

c. _____ We cannot **swallow** such a blow to our own self-respect.

d. _____ A minute ago, her cup was full, but now there are only a few **swallows** left.

CHECK ON PAGE 98

B. HOMONYMS AND HOMOGRAPHS

1.

> **Homonyms** are words with the same sounds but with different spellings and different meanings.
>   The wind **blew** away the clouds and left a **blue** sky above us.
> In this sentence, **blew** and **blue** are homonyms.
>   Everyone **stares** when the queen walks down the **stairs**.
> In this sentence, **stares** and **stairs** are **homonyms**.

Say each word and write it on the line next to the number. Then complete each sentence, using the words you wrote that sound like the words under the blanks in the sentence.

witch 19. _____

due 20. _____

eight 21. _____

knot 22. _____

threw 23. _____

weight 24. _____

tow 25. _____

Bare 26. _____

a. Winning the race was _____ to your help.
          do

b. Do you know how to tie a slip _____?
                      not

c. Long ago, a _____ might be put to death by burning.
              which

d. She gets up each morning at _____.
                     ate

e. He _____ the ball out of the window.
      through

f. They had to _____ the car away from the "No Parking" zone.
            toe

g. _____ feet are not allowed in the diner!
    Bear

h. She tries to throw her _____ around by giving orders to everyone!
                    wait

2.

> **Homographs** are words that have the same spelling but a different pronunciation and different meaning.
>   1. She tied the string into a pretty **bow**.
>   2. Everyone had to **bow** their heads before the king.
> In sentence 1, **bow** (bō) means a loop or a knot, and the word is used as a noun.
> In sentence 2, **bow** (bou) means to bend the head or body, and the word is used as a verb.
>   **Bow** (bō) and **bow** (bou) are homographs.

Say each word and write it on the line next to the number in the box. Then complete each sentence, using one of the words in the box. Place a check mark in the column to show whether the first syllable or the second syllable is accented. You may use a dictionary if you wish.

27. _____ present	28. _____ desert	29. _____ record	30. _____ permit

		Accent on first syllable	Accent on second syllable
i.	Where did you buy that new _____ player?		
j.	He said he could not _____ his friends during the fight.		
k.	Everyone was _____ at the meeting.		
l.	The sergeant ordered, "Attention! _____ arms!"		
m.	Have you seen the _____ in the American Southwest?		
n.	Tex and Billy Joe wanted to _____ their new song in our playroom.		
o.	I have no license, but I did get a learner's _____.		
p.	My dear, _____ me to drive you home.		

CHECK ON PAGE 98

C. SENTENCE PATTERNS

Two sentences, expressing two complete thoughts, are often joined by a **conjunction**. Sometimes the conjunction shows a **cause and its effect** and sometimes it shows a **reason and a result**.

The vegetables were turning red **because** they were ripe.
            1 effect   2 cause

Because the vegetables are ripe, they want to sell them at once.
            1 cause   2 effect

The vegetables, **because** they are ripe, should bring a good price.
   1 effect   2 cause   1 effect

Here are the conjunctions you know that show **cause and effect** or **reason and result**:

because   as   since   so   therefore

Read the longer sentences below. Circle the conjunction in each. Then decide which of the shorter sentences that make up the longer sentence shows cause or reason, and which shows effect or result. Write the number of the shorter sentence in the correct column.

	Cause or reason	Effect or result

a. It was difficult to say my prayers because
   <u>1</u>
   there was so much excitement outside.
   <u>2</u>

b. For thirty miles each way, the traffic is heavy; therefore,
   <u>1</u>
   we will have to drive slowly.
   <u>2</u>

c. Each village sent its workers and tools; thus
   <u>1</u>
   was the city built in the desert.
   <u>2</u>

d. I brought you two pounds of fresh cheese since
   <u>1</u>
   I knew you didn't like butter.
   <u>2</u>

e. I really don't like vegetable soup, so
   <u>1</u>
   I'll only eat a little bit.
   <u>2</u>

CHECK ON PAGE 98

D. SYLLABICATION/ACCENT

To unlock words that have two or more syllables, use the following steps:
1. Read the sentence for the word's meaning.
2. Divide the word into syllables.
3. Sound out the word, syllable by syllable.

Use these steps to try to figure out the word in dark print in the following sentence:

I read one **chapter** in the book.

First of all, read the sentence to learn about the word's meaning. From the sentence you can tell it is part of a book.

Second, divide the word into syllables like this: **chap-ter**.

Third, sound out the word syllable by syllable.

chap   The beginning sound is that of **ch** like in the word **child**. This is a closed syllable, so the **a** is probably short.

ter   The **t** sound is the same as that in the word **time**. The **er** is the same as that in **after**.

With all of these clues, you should have no trouble unlocking the word.

The words below the line might be new to you. Try to unlock each word. Then, on the line, write the word that belongs in each sentence.

1. There was a beautiful _____ in the sky.
   rainbow   ransom

2. We forgot to put _____ in the picnic basket.
   nicknames   napkins

3. That is my _____ story.
   federal   favorite

4. You should know the phone number of the nearest fire _____.
   department   desperate

5. You have my _____ to go.
   possession   permission

6. Because of all the noise, we couldn't _____.
   conference   concentrate

CHECK ON PAGE 98

A. WORDS IN SENTENCES

1. *Say each word and write it on the line next to the number. Then complete each sentence using the words you wrote.*

fuse   1. _____

crackle   2. _____

cord   3. _____

plug   4. _____

oil   5. _____

directions   6. _____

visitor   7. _____

salt   8. _____

screw   9. _____

knife   10. _____

wire   11. _____

flash   12. _____

bunch   13. _____

quite   14. _____

tight   15. _____

a.   I heard the _____ of electricity just before the _____ burned through and the _____ blew out.

b.   To change the _____, you must pull the _____ out of the tank.

c.   The _____ stopped at the service station to get _____.

d.   Please _____ on the top of the _____ shaker.

e.   That _____ is not sharp enough to cut the _____.

f.   The sheep stood together in a _____ because they were afraid of the _____ of lightning.

g.   I am not _____ sure why these shoes are so _____.

CHECK ON PAGE 99

DICTIONARY—ENTRIES

2. *Now study the four dictionary entries below. The meanings of the word in each entry depend on the way the word is used in a sentence. Match the definitions with one of the sentences at the right of the entry word by writing the number of the definition on the blank.*

1. **di rec tion** (də rek´shən),   **1** guiding; managing, control: *The school is under the direction of a good teacher.*   **2** order; command.   **3** knowing or telling what to do, how to do, or where to go; instruction: *He needs directions to the lake.*   **4** course taken by a moving body, such as a ball or a bullet.   **5** any way in which one may face or point. North, south east, and west are directions. *Our school is in one direction and the post office is in another.*   **6** course along which something moves; way of moving; tendency: *The town shows improvement in many directions.* noun.

a. _____ If I'm elected, our town will move in a new **direction**.

b. _____ Can you give me **directions** to Laughing Brook?

c. _____ Our office is now under the **direction** of Mr. Rivera.

d. _____ Which **direction** am I facing, north or south?

69

2. **flash** (flash),   **1** a sudden, brief light or flame: *a flash of lightning.*   **2** give out such a light or flame: *The lighthouse flashes signals twice a minute.*   **3** come suddenly; pass quickly: *A bird flashed across the road.*   **4** a sudden, short feeling or display: *a flash of hope.*   **5** a very short time: *It all happened in a flash.*   **6** give out or send out like a flash: *Her eyes flashed defiance.*
1, 4, 5 *noun, plural* **flash es; 2, 3, 6** *verb.*

a. _____ A falling star **flashed** across the night sky.

b. _____ There was a **flash** of light in the basement when I turned on the heat.

c. _____ I can **flash** my penlight to send the message.

d. _____ He saw the club in a **flash** just before the criminal hit him.

Notice that the word **fuse** *has two entries. First put the entry number (* **1** *or* **2** *), then the definition in that entry (* **1.1** *or* **1.2** *), to show the correct definition.*

3. **fuse**[1] (fyūz),   **1** part of an electric circuit that melts and breaks the circuit if the current becomes dangerously strong.   **2** a slow-burning wick or other device used to set off a shell, bomb, or blast of gunpowder.
   noun.
   fuse[2] (fyūz),   **1** melt; join together by melting: *Copper and zinc are fused to make brass.*   **2** blend; unite: *The intense heat fused the rocks together.*
   verb.

a. _____ The sergeant said, "Be sure to put a long **fuse** on that bomb!"

b. _____ He **fused** the two metals together when he repaired the broken bucket.

c. _____ The **fuse** blows out when there is too much electricity in the wires.

d. _____ The fire was so hot, it **fused** the glass and stones together.

4. **wire** (wīr),   **1** metal drawn out into a thread: *a telephone wire.*   **2** made of wire: *a wire fence.*   **3** furnish with wire: *wire a house for electricity.*   **4** fasten with wire: *He wired the two pieces together.*   **5** telegraph: *He sent a message by wire.*   **6** to telegraph: *He wired a birthday greeting.*   **7** telegram: *The news of his arrival came in a wire.*
1, 5, 7 *noun,* **2** *adjective,* **3, 4, 6** *verb,* **wired, wir ing.**

a. _____ A telegraph message used to be sent through a **wire**.

b. _____ He **wired** the doll's foot back onto its leg.

c. _____ We **wired** a message the day they were married.

d. _____ No cattle will break through this **wire** fence.

CHECK ON PAGE 99

B. ALPHABETICAL ORDER

Because the words in a dictionary are placed in **alphabetical order**, you will find the word **baggage** before the word **bait**. Both words have the same two letters at the beginning, *ba*, but the letter *g* in **baggage** comes before the letter *i* in **bait**.

To put words in alphabetical order:

1. Look at the first letter of the words, and put the words in alphabetical order by the first letter.

2. Look at all the words that begin with the same first letter. Put these words in order by the second letter.

3. Continue putting the words in order by the third letter, the fourth letter, and so on.

These words are in alphabetical order:

baby   baggage   bait   band   bar   bare   bath   battle

Explain why the word **bath** comes before the word **battle**.

Say each word and write it on the line next to the number. Put the four words into alphabetical order on the next group of lines. Then use one word from this group to complete each sentence.

	Words	Words in order

decide 16. _____ _____

desert 17. _____ _____

delicious 18. _____ _____

debt 19. _____ _____

a. The lunch was good, but the dinner was _____.

b. I hope I can find the money to pay that _____.

c. I couldn't _____ whether to swim or drown.

d. He doesn't seem like the kind of person who would _____ his family.

metal 20. _____ _____

medicine 21. _____ _____

meant 22. _____ _____

message 23. _____ _____

e. The doctor said that I should take the _____ three times a day.

f. I heard the _____ on the Citizens Band radio.

g. Many of the words were new to me, but I could tell what they _____.

h. The anchor of that ship is made of _____.

premium 24. _____ _____

prepare 25. _____ _____

predict 26. _____ _____

practice 27. _____ _____

i. He forgot to pay the _____ on his fire insurance.

j. That woman says she can _____ what will happen tomorrow.

k. I have to _____ the piano one hour each day.

l. It takes time to _____ such a good dinner.

CHECK ON PAGE 99

C. SENTENCE PATTERNS

Two sentences, expressing two complete thoughts, are often joined by conjunctions. Sometimes the conjunctions show a **contrast**, or a difference, between the ideas in each shorter sentence.

She has lived here for thirty years, **but** she cannot give good directions to a visitor.

Conjunctions that show contrast are:

although	but	however	in fact	instead
yet	on the other hand	otherwise	rather than	unlike

Sometimes the conjunctions show a **conclusion**.

Bob is unable to work with me, **so** we have little to say to each other.

Conjunctions that show a **conclusion** are:

so   so that   thus   therefore

71

Read each sentence. Circle the conjunction in each. Then make a check to show whether the second part of the sentence shows a contrast to the first part or a conclusion.

	Contrast	Conclusion

a. Many people think I have lived here forever; in fact, I have not.

b. The king and queen lived happily ever after; thus, our story comes to an end.

c. Pull out the blue cord so that there is no electricity in the record player.

d. The southern road is very busy, unlike the western road which is almost deserted.

e. That story is pleasant in the beginning, but it ends very unpleasantly for everyone.

f. The meat may have too much salt; on the other hand, it may have too little for some people's tastes.

g. The lights went out suddenly; therefore, I think the fuse has blown.

h. Rather than give the cake to Fred, I ate the whole thing myself!

CHECK ON PAGE 99

D. DICTIONARY PRONUNCIATION GUIDE

If you find that you cannot unlock a word, look it up in the dictionary. The dictionary shows the different sounds in a word by spelling the word in a special way. Next to each word in the dictionary, you can see its pronunciation. Here is an example:

type (tīp)

In the front and back of most dictionaries, you will find a **pronunciation key**. This key is a guide to the way letters are sounded when they are spoken in words. The pronunciation key shows you how letters sound when they come at the beginning, middle, or end of a word. You can see a full dictionary pronunciation key on page 124 of this book. Let's use this pronunciation key to sound out the word **type**.

To pronounce **type**, look at the special spelling. First there is a *t*. If you look at the pronunciation key, you'll see that the *t* sound can be found at the beginning of the word **tell** and at the end of the word **it**. Next you see an *i* with a bar over it. Looking again at the pronunciation key, you see that this is the long *i* sound as at the beginning of **ice** and in the middle of **five**. Last, there is a *p*. The pronunciation key tells you that this is the sound at the beginning of **paper** and at the end of **cup**. You should now have no trouble sounding out the word **type**.

You'll note that there are certain markings on letters in the pronunciation key. A bar over a vowel (ā) means it has the long sound; a vowel with no mark (i) has the short sound. You will also see dots and other markings. There's even an upside down *e* (ə) called a **schwa**. To see what sound each of these makes, just look at the guide words.

Below are the special dictionary spellings of some words. Use the pronunciation key to figure out each word and write the word on the blank line.

1. sôlt _____
2. kwīt _____
3. chēf _____
4. nīf _____
5. kyùr _____
6. kôf _____
7. nē _____
8. wīr _____
9. käm _____
10. tuf _____

CHECK ON PAGE 99

A. WORDS IN SENTENCES

1. *Say each word and write it on the line next to the number. Then complete each sentence using the words you wrote.*

museum   1. _____

several   2. _____

promise   3. _____

community   4. _____

arena   5. _____

polio   6. _____

disease   7. _____

slave   8. _____

cruel   9. _____

moan   10. _____

clinic   11. _____

x-ray   12. _____

guard   13. _____

library   14. _____

measles   15. _____

thorn   16. _____

limp   17. _____

a. Each year, _____ people _____ to give large gifts of money to repair our _____.

b. We are building a new sports _____ in the _____ center downtown.

c. Another terrible _____ that can be prevented is _____.

d. The _____ said he would not cry out or _____, no matter how _____ his owners were to him.

e. You can get a free _____ at the _____ on the corner.

f. The _____ will be closed today because the _____ has a bad case of _____.

g. She walked with a _____ because there was a _____ in her foot.

CHECK ON PAGE 100

DICTIONARY—ENTRIES

2. *Now study the four dictionary entries below. Match the number of the definition with the sentence at the right which uses the entry word to show the same meaning. Notice that entry number 3, **limp**, has two entries. First, put the entry number (**1** or **2**). Then put the number of the definition (**1.1** or **1.2**) to show the correct definition that matches the sentence.*

1. **com mu ni ty** (kə myü′nə tē),   **1** all the people living in the same place; the people of any district or town: *This lake provides water for six communities.*   **2** group of people living together or sharing common interests: *a community of monks, the scientific community.*   **3 the community**, the public: *To be successful a new product needs the approval of the community.*   **4** ownership together; sharing together: *community of food supplies.*
noun, plural **com mu ni ties.**

a. _____ We enjoy doing the same things together, so we have a **community** of interests.

b. _____ In our **community**, the sales tax is very high.

c. _____ When he got his new job, he felt he had joined the business **community**.

d. _____ The mayor asked her **community** to use less gas and oil.

2. **guard** (gärd),   **1** watch over; take care of; keep safe; defend: *The dog guarded the child day and night.*   **2** keep from escaping; check; hold back: *Guard the prisoners. Guard your tongue.*   **3** person or group that guards. A soldier or group of soldiers guarding a person or place is a guard.   **4** anything that gives protection; arrangement to give safety: *A fender is a guard against mud.*   **5** careful watch: *A soldier kept guard over the prisoners.*   **6** position of defense in boxing, fencing, and cricket.   **7** player at either side of the center in football.   **8** either of two players defending the goal in basketball.
1, 2 *verb,* **3–8** *noun.*

a. _____ The ball was passed to the **guard**, who shot from the side for a basket.

b. _____ An armed **guard** rode in the mayor's car.

c. _____ The men **guarded** the President's daughter until the criminals were caught.

d. _____ They **guard** the prison gate to keep the prisoners from escaping.

3. **limp**¹ (limp),   **1** a lame step or walk.   **2** walk with a limp: *After falling down the stairs, he limped for several days.*
1 *noun,* **2** *verb.*
limp² (limp),   not at all stiff; ready to bend or droop: *This starched collar soon gets limp in hot weather.*
adjective

a. _____ She **limped** for several days after she fell.

b. _____ The old soldier moved with a **limp**.

c. _____ The vegetables soon became **limp** in the hot sun.

d. _____ When she shook hands, her hand was **limp**.

4. **slave** (slāv),   **1** person who is the property of another. Slaves were once bought and sold like horses.   **2** person who is controlled or ruled by some desire, habit, or influence: *A drunkard is a slave of drink.*   **3** person who works like a slave.   **4** work like a slave: *Many mothers slave for their children.*   **5** of slaves; done by slaves: *slave labor.*
1–3 *noun,* **4** *verb,* **slaved, slav ing; 5** *adjective.*

a. _____ The **slaves** will rise up and take over that country.

b. _____ She **slaved** all day over the hot stove to make dinner for twenty-five people.

c. _____ Being afraid all the time has made her the **slave** of fear.

d. _____ Anyone who works fourteen hours a day, like you do, is a **slave** to the job!

CHECK ON PAGE 100

B. WORD MEANINGS

The words for the different parts of the body are **nouns** because they name something. Many of these words can also be used as **verbs**. They show actions like those which can be done by a part of the body.

Noun: That bear has a very cold **nose**.
Verb: It likes to **nose** around our cabin in the forest.

Noun: She kept her **eye** on the clock.
Verb: She **eyed** the broken glass sadly.

Say each word and write it on the line next to the number. Then complete each sentence, using one of the words at the left. A word may be used more than once. The clue under the blank space will help you choose the correct word.

paw 18. _____

knee 19. _____

chest 20. _____

skin 21. _____

ankle 22. _____

finger 23. _____

elbow 24. _____

neck 25. _____

a. When the monster was angry, it pounded on its

_____.
(ends like best)

b. The lion had a thorn in its _____.
(animal's hand, or foot)

c. Her dress comes down to her _____.
(lets you fold your leg)

d. Mother told us not to _____ the vegetables
(handle)

before we bought them.

e. The hunter took a long time to _____ the animal.
(take off the fur)

f. If you keep your nose in the air, you'll get a sore

_____.
(ends like wreck)

g. The water is so low in that river, it only comes up to my

_____.
(joins the foot to the leg)

h. During the rush hour, she has to _____ her way
(lets the arm fold up)

through the crowd.

i. "Mr. Mouth" put the _____ on those criminals,
(where you wear a ring)

and they were arrested.

stomach 26. _____

wrist 27. _____

hip 28. _____

shoulder 29. _____

j. His daughter's head only comes up to his _____.
(ends like ship)

k. I can't _____ the way he acts.
(food fills it)

l. If you pretend not to see someone, you are giving them a "cold _____."
(ends like older)

m. After a big meal, there's no room in your _____.
(food fills it)

n. To play tennis well, you need a strong _____.
(joins the hand to the arm)

CHECK ON PAGE 100

C. SENTENCE PATTERNS

> Two complete sentences, expressing two complete thoughts, are often joined into one sentence by a **conjunction**. Some conjunctions, like **so** and **so that**, are used to show **purpose**. They tell **why**.
>
> Give money to our clinic **so that** we can fight disease.
>
> Other conjunctions, like **if**, **whether**, and **unless**, are used to show condition—one or more things must happen before something else can happen.
>
> You can help the community **if** you give money to build the new library.

1. *Read the sentences below. Circle the conjunctions. Then put a check in the correct box to show whether the sentence shows a **purpose** or a **condition**.*

	Purpose	Condition
a.		
b.		
c.		
d.		
e.		

a. Whether she has had polio or not, she walks with a small limp.

b. If you want to help the library, you must return your books on time.

c. You may get sick too, unless you have already had the measles.

d. Hold still so that the x-ray of your chest will be clear.

e. You must pay the fine; otherwise, you can't take out any more books.

2. *Read the sentences below that were made from several small sentences. Circle each conjunction you see. Then write the conjunction after the word that tells what job it does in the sentence. The first one has been done for you.*

a. The last bus was crowded; however, we were willing to stand, even if we couldn't get a seat, so that we would get home in time for the wedding.

contrast: *however*   **condition**: *even if*   **purpose**: *so that*

b. Whenever all the seats are taken, Ginny pretends to be very tired or she pretends to be sick until someone gets up and offers to give her a seat.

time: _____ _____   **new idea**: _____ _____

c. Since we had fifty miles to travel before we got home, we each took a book to read and some food to eat too.

time: _____   **new idea**: _____   **reason or cause**: _____

d. Although the roads were crowded and the rain was freezing as it fell, we made good time; that is, we took only two hours longer than usual.

example: _____   **new idea**: _____   **contrast**: _____

CHECK ON PAGE 100

D. UNLOCKING NEW WORDS

In words with two or more syllables, one syllable will be stressed more than others. This syllable is called the **accented syllable** and is marked in the dictionary with an **accent mark** (´). Say the following words, putting the accent on the correct syllable:

moment (mo´ mənt)
detective (di tek´ tiv)

Divide each word into syllables and write the divided word on the blank line. Then circle the accented syllable.

1. ankle _____
2. music _____
3. swallow _____
4. excitement _____
5. dangerous _____
6. infection _____

CHECK ON PAGE 100

REVIEW 26–30

Say each word and write it on the line next to the number. Then complete each part by writing one word on each blank line. The numbers under the lines tell you which words to choose from.

A.

1. _____ clinic
2. _____ library
15. _____ comfortable
16. _____ fourth

3. _____ museum
4. _____ community
17. _____ difficult
18. _____ delicious

5. _____ Chief
6. _____ Several
19. _____ cord
20. _____ disease

7. _____ imagine
8. _____ flash
21. _____ infection
22. _____ arena

9. _____ practice
10. _____ bath
23. _____ carriers
24. _____ mayors

11. _____ decided
12. _____ moaned
25. _____ plug
26. _____ prevent

13. _____ metal
14. _____ medicine
27. _____ spy
28. _____ guard

I'm a doctor in a _____ in a poor _____. _____ of my friends
　　　　　　　　　　(1 or 2)　　　　　　　　　(3 or 4)　　　　　　　　(5 or 6)

can't _____ why I would give up my private _____ to work here. I tell them that I
　　　　(7 or 8)　　　　　　　　　　　　　　　　　　　(9 or 10)

_____ to study _____ to help people, not to make a _____ living.
　(11 or 12)　　　　　　(13 or 14)　　　　　　　　　　　　　　　(15 or 16)

But I must admit that working in this clinic is more _____ than I had thought.
　　　　　　　　　　　　　　　　　　　　　　　　　(17 or 18)

There is a great deal of _____ here. Because of the poor conditions, it's easy for one person
　　　　　　　　　　　　(19 or 20)

to give another an _____. Many times people don't even know they are _____
　　　　　　　　　(21 or 22)　　　　　　　　　　　　　　　　　　　　　　　　(23 or 24)

until they have given their disease to others. To _____ this, I urge people to get checkups and
　　　　　　　　　　　　　　　　　　　　　　(25 or 26)

tell them how to _____ against infection.
　　　　　　　(27 or 28)

B.

29. _____
fat

30. _____
national

41. _____
cheese

42. _____
desert

31. _____
chest

32. _____
pleasant

43. _____
cow

44. _____
butter

33. _____
ankle

34. _____
dinner

45. _____
wire

46. _____
vegetables

35. _____
gravy

36. _____
thorns

47. _____
cruel

48. _____
flat

37. _____
bricks

38. _____
potatoes

49. _____
aim

50. _____
snake

39. _____
salt

40. _____
polio

51. _____
guide

52. _____
promise

One day a _____ man named Roy came here with _____ pains. After
        (29 or 30)   (31 or 32)

checking him over, I told Roy to lose weight.

"What do you eat for _____?" I asked.
                   (33 or 34)

"I like meat with plenty of _____ and _____," he said. "Many times I put
             (35 or 36)   (37 or 38)

extra _____ on my food at the table. I also like to eat _____. After the main
     (39 or 40)   (41 or 42)

course, I have cake and coffee."

"Cut down on red meat and salt," I suggested. "Baked potatoes are fine, but without _____.
                                                      (43 or 44)

Cut out the cheese and gravy, and eat some _____. And replace the cake with fruit.
                                      (45 or 46)

"Dr. Moreno, you're _____," Roy said.
                    (47 or 48)

"No," I replied. "My _____ is to prevent a heart attack. I want you to _____
             (49 or 50)   (51 or 52)

you'll lose weight." And he did.

C.

53. _____
western

54. _____
x-ray

63. _____
coach

64. _____
mate

55. _____
bit

56. _____
bunch

65. _____
visitor

66. _____
college

57. _____
sex

58. _____
wrist

67. _____
Teammates

68. _____
Slaves

59. _____
wagons

60. _____
elbows

69. _____
prediction

70. _____
excitement

61. _____
shoulders

62. _____
witches

71. _____
imagination

72. _____
knife

The _____ machine had a busy day when a _____ of basketball players got
(53 or 54)   (55 or 56)

into a fight. I treated one broken _____, two broken _____, and four wounded
                                   (57 or 58)   (59 or 60)

_____.
(61 or 62)

    The _____ told me that basketball is important to the young players because they
           (63 or 64)

see it as a way to get to _____, and maybe the good life. _____ stand up for each
                          (65 or 66)   (67 or 68)

other, sometimes getting carried away by the _____ of the game. That's how the fight started.
                                             (69 or 70)

    I hope one of the players I treated becomes a famous basketball star one day. In my _____,
                                                                                        (71 or 72)

I like to picture the good life for all these young people.

D.

73. _____
measles

74. _____
screws

83. _____
appeared

84. _____
repeated

75. _____
fuses

76. _____
coughs

85. _____
swallowed

86. _____
skinned

77. _____
hardship

78. _____
oil

87. _____
paw

88. _____
pulse

79. _____
fought

80. _____
ought

89. _____
finger

90. _____
stomach

81. _____
quite

82. _____
tight

91. _____
prayer

92. _____
dream

The children touch me the most. I've treated many cases of _____, _____,
(73 or 74)   (75 or 76)

and broken bones. These are problems that all children face. But here, children face _____ that
(77 or 78)

no child _____ to suffer.
(79 or 80)

Last month a little girl named Tina was _____ sick when she was brought into my clinic. It
(81 or 82)

_____ that she had _____ some drugs someone had left around the house. Her
(83 or 84)   (85 or 86)

_____ was very faint, and I knew I would have to get the drugs out of her _____
(87 or 88)   (89 or 90)

fast. I said a silent _____ and went to work.
(91 or 92)

Luck was with me and Tina pulled through, but I can't tell you how many children I've lost.

E.

93. _____   94. _____   99. _____   100. _____
         ripe   peaceful   excite   predict

95. _____   96. _____   101. _____   102. _____
      temperature   crackle   cure   limp

97. _____   98. _____   103. _____   104. _____
         nation   hip   themselves   direction

Well, today has been pretty _____ here—so far nothing worse than a baby with a
(93 or 94)

_____ and an old woman with pain in her _____. But I _____ that
(95 or 96)   (97 or 98)   (99 or 100)

we'll get very busy before the day is over.

I wish I could _____ everyone who comes in here, but I can't. It gets to me at times. I just
(101 or 102)

turned sixty-eight, and sometimes I think it's time to quit. But then again, if these people won't quit on

_____, I'm not going to be the one to desert them.
(103 or 104)

CHECK ON PAGE 101

81

Language Clues Spelling Words

CA-16 Lesson Words

1. ate
2. bowl
3. built
4. cattle
5. crop
6. destroy
7. drift
8. dry
9. feed
10. plain
11. prairie
12. receive
13. root
14. service
15. tow
16. town
17. vacation
18. wheat
19. cracks
20. coughing

Review Words

1. simplest
2. angrier
3. dirtiest
4. earlier
5. palest
6. fainter
7. faintest
8. friendlier
9. richer
10. highest
11. taller
12. steadier
13. lighter
14. angriest
15. bravest
16. healthier
17. kindest
18. louder
19. meanest
20. noisier

CA-17 Lesson Words

1. baby
2. bucket
3. cheap
4. cloth
5. dent
6. dizzy
7. forty
8. guy
9. hood
10. lemon
11. motor
12. rattle
13. sharp
14. stray
15. surprise
16. tough
17. vehicle
18. waste
19. eyelid
20. dream
21. rapid

Review Words

1. ashamed
2. stirring
3. plowed
4. challenging
5. driven
6. joins
7. shaped
8. tasting
9. wiped
10. chews
11. drawing
12. allowed
13. pointing
14. understands
15. pretended

CA-18 Lesson Words

1. bar
2. bare
3. bark
4. candy
5. dock
6. extra
7. jail
8. leather
9. pet
10. puppy
11. reward
12. rug
13. ruin
14. sailor
15. shoe
16. spear
17. swim
18. wander

Review Words

1. bounces
2. parties
3. nurses
4. services
5. babies
6. surprises
7. vehicles
8. wastes
9. crimes
10. tunes
11. plates
12. wines
13. nests
14. prints
15. shovels
16. trees
17. facts
18. laws
19. camps
20. bands
21. knots
22. prisons
23. bowls
24. dreams

CA-19 Lesson Words

1. action
2. army
3. arrive
4. bottom
5. crack
6. kneel
7. lend
8. mouse
9. pressure
10. rifle
11. sir
12. sixty
13. success
14. suggest
15. suppose
16. trap
17. warn
18. wound

Review Words

1. puppy
2. dizzy
3. rattle
4. cattle
5. manner
6. matter
7. teeth
8. allow
9. tall
10. tree
11. address
12. application
13. written
14. message
15. married
16. wedding
17. tool
18. disappoint
19. waitress
20. terrible

CA-20 Lesson Words

1. anchor
2. bridge
3. cheer
4. disturb
5. except
6. folks
7. forward
8. material
9. mistake
10. permit
11. refuse
12. respect
13. ocean
14. thousand
15. trust
16. welcome
17. wet
18. yard

Review Words

1. renumber
2. reelection
3. report
4. reload
5. retool
6. rediscover
7. regain
8. remarried
9. reform
10. reprint
11. refasten
12. return
13. rework
14. refresh
15. review
16. redraw

CA-21 Lesson Words

1. alcohol
2. become
3. became
4. blaze
5. court
6. dozen
7. foreman
8. Friday
9. fumes
10. private
11. relax
12. repair
13. shock
14. silent
15. silence
16. silly
17. smash
18. student
19. stupid
20. grand

Review Words

1. different
2. attractive
3. beautiful
4. breakable
5. dangerous
6. experimental
7. laughable
8. lonely
9. national
10. northeastern
11. peaceful
12. pleasant
13. suitable
14. southwestern
15. worthless
16. wonderful

CA-22 Lesson Words

1. alley
2. blanket
3. growl
4. human
5. insurance
6. notice
7. pen
8. pencil
9. policy
10. premium
11. prepare
12. rag
13. remain
14. repeat
15. reply
16. secret
17. thirsty
18. treat
19. uncle
20. daughters
21. grand

Review Words

1. receive
2. record (verb)
3. refuse
4. report
5. remember
6. present (verb)
7. pretend
8. preview
9. reward
10. return
11. respect
12. review
13. agency
14. depend
15. detective
16. election
17. famous
18. grocery
19. idea
20. motor
21. Negro
22. open
23. follow
24. hello
25. paper
26. private
27. radar
28. piano
29. station
30. stolen
31. window

CA-23 Lesson Words
1. bite
2. clever
3. closet
4. collar
5. curb
6. flag
7. judge
8. license
9. manage
10. neck
11. shadow
12. travel
13. truth
14. urge
15. wag
16. wagged
17. whether
18. wise
19. leash

Review Words
1. baking
2. blazing
3. caring
4. changing
5. daring
6. clubbing
7. cutting
8. fanning
9. forgetting
10. grabbing
11. gambling
12. imagining
13. overcoming
14. practicing
15. wrestling

CA-24 Lesson Words
1. baggage
2. calm
3. collect
4. couple
5. cream
6. debt
7. due
8. interest
9. January
10. knee
11. meant
12. payment
13. polite
14. puzzle
15. red
16. shy
17. stare
18. yellow
19. canoe
20. paddle
21. rise
22. jacket

Review Words
1. January
2. February
3. March
4. April
5. May
6. June
7. July
8. August
9. September
10. October
11. November
12. December
13. Sunday
14. Monday
15. Tuesday
16. Wednesday
17. Thursday
18. Friday
19. Saturday

CA-25 Lesson Words
1. apply
2. arrest
3. barrel
4. citizen
5. criminal
6. dangerous
7. discharge
8. fought
9. handle
10. height
11. illness
12. inches
13. replace
14. spy
15. theater
16. unable
17. unemployed
18. zone
19. President

Review Words
1. unexpected
2. unclean
3. unhappy
4. unlucky
5. unsafe
6. about
7. above
8. across
9. adult
10. again
11. around
12. amount
13. unsteady
14. unchanged
15. undecided
16. uneasy
17. unhurt
18. unimportant

CA-26 Lesson Words
1. aim
2. carrier
3. chief
4. coach
5. college
6. flat
7. fourth
8. hardship
9. imagination
10. imagine
11. mate
12. nation
13. national
14. ought
15. peaceful
16. predict
17. prediction
18. themselves

Review Words
1. criminal
2. payment
3. dangerous
4. vacation
5. township
6. condition
7. application
8. employment
9. invention
10. experimental
11. business
12. election
13. government
14. likeness
15. restful
16. wonderful

CA-27 Lesson Words
1. appear
2. bath
3. comfortable
4. cough
5. cure
6. dinner
7. dream
8. fat
9. gravy
10. infection
11. medicine
12. pleasant
13. potato
14. prevent
15. pulse
16. sex
17. skin
18. temperature

Review Words
1. written
2. wrestling
3. wagged
4. unemployed
5. weight
6. suggesting
7. surprising
8. remembering
9. predicted
10. promised
11. managed
12. licensing
13. happened
14. governed
15. discharged
16. disappointing

CA-28 Lesson Words
1. bit
2. brick
3. butter
4. cheese
5. cow
6. desert
7. decide
8. difficult
9. excite
10. excitement
11. guide
12. prayer
13. ripe
14. snake
15. swallow
16. vegetable
17. wagon
18. western
19. mayor
20. witch

Review Words
1. red/read
2. shoe/shoo
3. pail/pale
4. board/bored
5. sent/cent
6. eye/I
7. here/hear
8. there/their
9. male/mail
10. meat/meet
11. nose/knows
12. peace/piece
13. plain/plane
14. toe/tow

CA-29 Lesson Words
1. bunch
2. cord
3. crackle
4. delicious
5. direction
6. flash
7. fuse
8. knife
9. metal
10. oil
11. plug
12. practice
13. quite
14. salt
15. screw
16. tight
17. visitor
18. wire

Review Words
1. calf
2. calves
3. half
4. halves
5. wolf
6. wolves
7. loaf
8. loaves
9. knife
10. knives
11. herself
12. themselves
13. child
14. children
15. chick
16. chicken
17. chickens
18. tooth
19. teeth
20. foot
21. feet
22. woman
23. women
24. man
25. men

CA-30 Lesson Words
1. chest
2. clinic
3. community
4. cruel
5. disease
6. guard
7. library
8. limp
9. measles
10. moan
11. museum
12. paw
13. polio
14. promise
15. several
16. slave
17. thorn
18. x-ray
19. ankle
20. elbow
21. finger
22. hip
23. shoulder
24. stomach
25. wrist

Review Words
1. before
2. meanwhile
3. until
4. whenever
5. while
6. because
7. therefore
8. since
9. example
10. furthermore
11. also
12. thus
13. however
14. although
15. instead
16. whether

ANSWER KEY
CA-16

A.

1.
1. plain	a. built	cattle
2. built	plain	
3. cattle		

4. cracks	b. dry	roots
5. dry	cracks	
6. roots		

| 7. coughing | c. coughing | drift |
| 8. drift | | |

9. service	d. tow	town
10. tow	service	
11. town		

2.

1.	a. 1	2.	a. 3
	b. 2		b. 1
	c. 4		c. 5
	d. 3		d. 6

3.	a. 2	4.	a. 1
	b. 4		b. 3
	c. 5		c. 1
	d. 1		d. 2

B.

12. ate	a. ate	ate
13. receive	b. receive	bowl
14. destroy	c. destroy	crop
		destroy
15. prairie	d. wheat	feed
16. wheat	e. crop	prairie
17. crop	f. prairie	receive
		vacation
18. vacation	g. feed	wheat
19. Bowl	h. Bowl	
20. feed	i. vacation	

C.

1.
  a. Oh, or Why
  b. Now, Well, or Oh
  c. Oh, Well, or Why
  d. Why, Well, or Oh

2.
  a. No,
  b. Say,
  c. Yes,
  d. Listen,

D.

1. a. yet
   b. yourself
   c. yell
2. a. dry
   b. fly
   c. sky
3. a. gray
   b. play
   c. subway
4. a. factory
   b. bury
   c. duty

A.

1. 1. cloth   a. bucket   cheap
   2. bucket   cloth
   3. cheap

   4. dizzy   b. baby   dizzy
   5. baby

   6. tough   c. guy   tough
   7. guy

   8. stray   d. surprise   stray
   9. surprise

   10. eyelid   e. sharp   eyelid
   11. sharp

   12. rapid   f. rapid   dream
   13. dream

- -

2.

1.	a. 1		2.	a. 1
	b. 2			b. 8
	c. 1			c. 9
	d. 3			d. 4

3.	a. 4		4.	a. 4
	b. 3			b. 3
	c. 1			c. 2
	d. 5			d. 6

B.

14. motor   a. Check   motor
15. lemon.   lemon.
16. Check

17. Where   b. Where   dent
18. hood?   hood?
19. dent

20. money!   c. vehicle   waste
21. waste   money!
22. vehicle

23. windows   d. forty   windows
24. rattle.   rattle.
25. forty

C.

a. Doesn't   d. wouldn't
b. not   e. not
c. can't   f. Aren't

D.

1. 1   6. 3
2. 2   7. 1
3. 2   8. 2
4. 3   9. 2
5. 1   10. 3

CA-18

A.

1.
1. bare   a. rug   bare
2. rug

3. pet   b. reward   pet
4. reward

5. extra   c. extra   bars
6. bars   jail
7. jail

8. dock   d. sailor   wandered
9. sailor   dock
10. wandered

11. swim   e. spear   swim
12. spear

2.

1.			2.		
a.	3		a.	1	
b.	1		b.	4	
c.	2		c.	3	
d.	4		d.	2	

3.			4.		
a.	1		a.	1	
b.	2		b.	2	
c.	4		c.	3	
d.	3		d.	1	

B.

13. reddish   a. bark   reddish
14. bark

15. candy   b. candy   childish
16. childish

17. purplish   c. leather   purplish
18. leather

19. puppy   d. puppy   puppyish
20. puppyish

21. foolish   e. ruin   foolish
22. ruin

23. shoes   f. shoes   brownish
24. brownish

C.

a. Who   d. What
b. When   e. How or When
c. Why   f. Where

D.

1.
a. cat tle   f. suf fer
b. pup py   g. writ ten
c. al low   h. ad dress
d. mar ry   i. mat ter
e. rat tle   j. rub ber

2.
a. wan der   f. plat form
b. cap tain   g. con trol
c. can cer   h. ad mit
d. slen der   i. cer tain
e. pow der   j. per son

CA-19

A.

1.
1. pressure	a. trap	pressure
2. mouse		mouse
3. trap		
4. crack	b. kneel	bottom
5. kneel		crack
6. bottom		
7. rifle	c. rifle	warn
8. warn		
9. wound	d. lend	wound
10. lend		

- -

2.

1.	a. 1	2.	a. 1
	b. 5		b. 5
	c. 3		c. 3
	d. 4		d. 2

3.	a. 1	4.	a. ___ b. ✔
	b. 2		✔ ___
	c. 5		___ ✔
	d. 1		✔ ___

B.

11. allow	action	a. action
12. arrive	adventure	b. adventure
13. army	allow	c. allow
14. adventure	army	d. arrive
15. action	arrive	e. army
16. success	sir	f. sixty
17. suppose	sixty	g. suggest
18. suggest	success	h. suppose
19. sir	suggest	i. sir
20. sixty	suppose	j. success

C.

a. Will	hear the shot
b. Could	clean out that wound
c. Should	walk on the other side of the street
d. Wasn't	ready when you shot the rifle
e. Has	you to come today

D.

1. (bas)(ket)
2. (in) (vent)
3. e (ven)
4. a go
5. (suc) (cess)
6. be (long)
7. (hel) lo
8. (sug) (gest)
9. ra (dar)
10. de gree

A.

1.
1. ocean   a. anchor   ocean
2. anchor   thousand
3. thousand

4. cheer   b. cheer   forward
5. bridge   bridge
6. forward

7. folks   c. disturb   folks
8. except   except
9. disturb

10. welcome   d. trust   permit
11. trust   welcome
12. permit

13. material   e. material   yard
14. yard

15. wet   f. mistake   wet
16. mistake

2.

1.			2.	
a.	2		a.	2
b.	1		b.	5
c.	3		c.	4
d.	4		d.	1

3.			4.	
a.	2		a.	1 ✔ pər mit′
b.	5		b.	2
c.	1			✔ per′mit
d.	4			

B.

17. respected 19. replace 21. recount
18. reelection 20. refused 22. rejoin

	Re means again	Re means back	Re does NOT mean again or back
a. refused			✔
b. recount	✔		
c. replace		✔	
d. respected			✔
e. rejoin	✔		
f. reelection	✔		

C.

a. Does
b. Don't
c. Didn't
d. Did
e. Doesn't

D.

1. ex/tra
2. mon/ster
3. kit/chen
4. weath/er
5. sur/prise
6. re/spect

Review Lesson
16-20

A.

1. dream
2. crop
3. anchor
4. eyelid
5. forty
6. sixty
7. mistake
8. thousand
9. folks
10. cattle
11. wet
12. extra
13. feed
14. dry
15. yard
16. shoe
17. dizzy
18. welcome
19. arrive
20. receive

The words in the paragraphs are:

dream   eyelid   sixty   mistake   folks
extra   feed   shoe   welcome   arrive

B.

21. sailor
22. puppy
23. stray
24. mouse
25. army
26. town
27. bucket
28. pet
29. bark
30. cheer
31. ruin
32. wound
33. ate
34. built
35. bar
36. bowl
37. lend
38. destroy
39. permit
40. trap

The words in the paragraphs are:

puppy   stray   town   pet   bark   ruin
ate   bowl   destroy   permit

C.

41. crack
42. prairie
43. dent
44. dock
45. ocean
46. hood
47. baby
48. motor
49. rattle
50. rug
51. reward
52. disturb
53. rapid
54. cheap
55. vehicle
56. bridge
57. bare
58. sharp
59. surprise
60. success

The words in the paragraphs are:

crack   dent   hood   motor   rattle
disturb   cheap   vehicle   sharp   surprise

D.

61. vacation
62. drift
63. pressure
64. cloth
65. spear
66. leather
67. bottom
68. tough
69. warn
70. waste
71. wander
72. suggest
73. sir
74. guy

The words in the paragraphs are:

vacation   pressure   leather   tough   warn
suggest   sir

E.

75. material
76. service
77. root
78. plain
79. wheat
80. lemon
81. candy
82. rifle
83. trust
84. respect
85. jail
86. coughing
87. forward
88. except
89. action
90. swim
91. kneel
92. refuse
93. suppose
94. tow

The words in the paragraphs are:

service   plain   lemon   candy   trust
coughing   forward   action   refuse
suppose

CA-21

A.

1.
1. private   a. Friday   private
2. relax   relax
3. Friday

4. silence   b. silent   silence
5. silent   silly
6. silly

7. shock   c. blaze   students
8. students   shock
9. blaze

10. alcohol   d. smash   alcohol
11. smash

12. dozen   e. dozen   repair
13. court   court
14. repair

15. fumes   f. fumes   stupid
16. stupid

- -

2.

1.	a.	2
	b.	1
	c.	3
	d.	5

2.	a.	1
	b.	4
	c.	1
	d.	5

3.	a.	5
	b.	2
	c.	4
	d.	1

4.	a.	1
	b.	7
	c.	2
	d.	6

B.

17. become   a. be/come   fore/man
18. foreman

19. bareback   b. be/came   bare/back
20. became

21. motorboat   c. swim/suit   motor/boat
22. swimsuit

23. doorway   d. door/way   back/yard
24. backyard

25. aftershock   e. earth/quake
26. earthquake   after/shock

27. touchdown   f. grand/stand
28. grandstand   full/back   touch/down
29. fullback

C.

a. (In) the king's court (at) noon
   where   when
b. (down) the stairs (into) the hall
   where   where
c. (Before) the party (to) the store
   when   where
d. (With) an angry look (on) the table
   how   where
e. (by) a trick (before) the whole court
   how   where
f. (of) my father's (after) the football game
   which   when

D.

1. stu dent   6. pre tend
2. de pend   7. o cean
3. e lect   8. re ceive
4. be came   9. stu pid
5. fa mous   10. mo tor

CA-22

A.

1.
1. alley   a. growl   alley
2. growl

3. repeat   b. repeat   secret
4. secret

5. treat   c. thirsty   treat
6. thirsty

7. blanket   d. blanket   rag
8. rag

9. insurance   e. notice   insurance
10. notice

11. remain   f. policy   remain
12. policy

13. pen   g. pen   premium
14. premium

15. pencil   h. pencil   human
16. human

17. reply   i. prepare   reply
18. prepare

2.

1.		2.	
a.	2	a.	4
b.	3	b.	2
c.	1	c.	5
d.	1	d.	2

3.		4.	
a.	2	a.	3
b.	1	b.	1
c.	3	c.	6
d.	1	d.	8

B.

19. uncle   a. great-uncle
20. sixty   sixty-eight

21. birth   b. great-grandfather
22. grandfather   birthday

23. grandmother   c. great-grandmother
24. daughter   granddaughter

25. aunt   d. great-aunt
26. sister   sister-in-law

27. grandson   e. great-grandson
28. Fifty   Fifty-first

29. brother   f. brother-in-law
30. second   fifty-second

C.

1.
a. (Angela)
    was drawn by (Angela)
b. (The man)
    is heard by (the man)
c. (My mother)
    be bought by (my mother)
d. (The doctor)
    was read by (the doctor)
e. (anyone)
    be paid by (anyone)

2.
a. was made in secret
b. repeated the lesson
c. The old blanket was torn into rags
d. find that book inside the car

D.

1. man ner   closed
2. blan ket   closed
3. se cret   open
4. re main   open
5. an gry   closed
6. si lent   open
7. ex cept   closed

CA-23

A.

1.
| 1. neck | a. collar | neck |
| 2. collar | | |

3. license	b. curb	judge
4. curb	license	
5. judge		

| 6. bite | c. wagged | bite |
| 7. wagged | | |

| 8. urge | d. urge | flag |
| 9. flag | | |

| 10. travel | e. travel | closet |
| 11. closet | | |

12. manage	f. whether	manage
13. wag	wag	
14. whether		

2.

1.	a. 1		2.	a. 2
	b. 2			b. 1
	c. 6			c. 3
	d. 9			d. 1

3.	a. 2		4.	a. 5
	b. 1			b. 3
	c. 1			c. 1
	d. 3			d. 2

B.

1.
15. repair	a. smash
16. remain	b. remain
17. prepare	c. leash
18. reply	d. reply
19. smash	e. repair
20. leash	f. prepare

2.
21. clever	g. shadow
22. wise	h. backward
23. shadow	i. clever
24. truth	j. truth
25. backward	k. wise

C.

a. to stay home, (not) to travel.
b. opened his shirt collar (and) rubbed his neck.
c. opened the closet (and) took out my shirt.
d. the desk (or) the chairs.
e. a bowl of soup (and) a glass of milk.

D.

1. li cense	6. hu man
2. trav el	7. no tice
3. riv er	8. rap id
4. re peat	9. lem on
5. doz en	10. pre pare

A.

1.
1. paddle   a. paddle   canoe
2. canoe

3. jacket   b. cream   jacket
4. cream

5. knee   c. couple   knee
6. couple

7. red   d. yellow   red
8. rise   rise
9. yellow

10. shy   e. shy   stare
11. stare

2.

1.		2.	
a.	3	a.	3
b.	1	b.	4
c.	2	c.	5
d.	1	d.	1

3.		4.	
a.	3	a.	1
b.	5	b.	3
c.	8	c.	2
d.	2	d.	1

B.

12. September   a. debt   due
13. debt   Tuesday   September
14. due
15. Tuesday

16. baggage   b. polite   baggage
17. Thursday   Thursday
18. polite

19. collect   c. collect   interest
20. interest   February
21. February

22. Saturday   d. puzzle   meant
23. meant   Saturday
24. puzzle

25. Wednesday   e. calm   Wednesday
26. October   October
27. calm

28. January   f. payment   December
29. payment   January
30. December

C.

a. After they found his baggage, he became calm again.
b. She dropped her eyes because she was shy.
c. Today is Tuesday so we must make the first payment on our debt.
d. The flag was red at the top and there was some yellow at the bottom.
e. When the canoe turned over, we lost our paddle.

D.

1. pad dle   6. scram ble
2. sim ple   7. strad dle
3. trou ble   8. rat tle
4. mid dle   9. ta ble
5. bat tle   10. cou ple

CA-25

A.

1.
1. replace   a. barrel   replace
2. handle   handle
3. barrel

4. spy   b. citizen   spy
5. citizen

6. zone   c. inches   zone
7. inches

8. discharge   d. discharge   illness
9. illness

10. arrest   e. criminal   arrest
11. criminal

2.

1.	a. 3
	b. 1
	c. 4
	d. 2

2.	a. 7
	b. 5
	c. 6
	d. 3

3.	a. 3
	b. 6
	c. 1
	d. 4

4.	a. 3
	b. 1
	c. 2
	d. 1

B.

12. disturbed   a. President   disturbed
13. undisturbed
14. President

15. apply   b. unemployed   apply
16. employed
17. unemployed

18. adrift   c. dangerous   adrift
19. astray
20. dangerous

21. theater   d. unable   theater
22. able
23. unable

24. easy   e. height   uneasy
25. uneasy
26. height

27. fought   f. ashamed   fought
28. ashamed
29. unashamed

C.

1.
a. My father
b. Looking for a new job
c. The barrel
d. Gwen
   Gwen
e. The citizens
   The spy
   The spy

2.
a. policeman (who)
b. illness (that)
c. truck (that)
d. man (who)
e. theater in (which)
f. horse (which)

D.

1. unhappy
2. reread
3. repay
4. unwilling
5. displeased
6. unemployed
7. disorder
8. dishonor
9. unable
10. rebuilt

94

Review Lesson
21–25

A.

1. knee
2. alcohol
3. growl
4. handle
5. unemployed
6. wise
7. daughter
8. citizen
9. fumes
10. private
11. relax
12. refuse
13. policy
14. truth
15. unsafe
16. unable

The words in the paragraphs are:

alcohol   handle   unemployed   daughter
private   relax   truth   unable

B.

17. manage
18. replace
19. debt
20. secret
21. became
22. spied
23. clever
24. yellow
25. notice
26. prepare
27. paddled
28. fought
29. canoe
30. theater
31. silly
32. shy
33. wag
34. stare
35. polite
36. red
37. remain
38. rise
39. puzzled
40. meant
41. reply
42. shock
43. uncle
44. silence

The words in the paragraphs are:

manage   secret   became   clever   notice
fought   theater   silly   stare   polite
remain   meant   reply   silence

C.

45. Friday
46. curb
47. zone
48. January
49. blaze
50. travel
51. dozen
52. premium
53. closet
54. barrel
55. collect
56. bite
57. pencil
58. jacket

59. payment
60. due
61. students
62. baggage
63. insurance
64. interest
65. rag
66. blanket
67. calm
68. stupid
69. dangerous
70. grand
71. smashed
72. wagged

The words in the paragraphs are:

Friday   January   travel   dozen   closet
collect   jacket   due   students   interest
blanket   stupid   dangerous   smashed

D.

73. cream
74. arrest
75. criminal
76. president
77. inches
78. court
79. judge
80. aunt
81. license
82. leash
83. collared
84. urged
85. neck
86. whether
87. silent
88. lonely
89. become
90. shadowed
91. repeat
92. repair

The words in the paragraphs are:

arrest   criminal   court   judge   license
urged   whether   silent   become   repair

E.

93. human
94. foreman
95. thirsty
96. height
97. pen
98. couple
99. illness
100. alley
101. flag
102. treat
103. discharge
104. apply

The words in the paragraphs are:

human   thirsty   couple   illness   treat
apply

CA-26

A.

1.
1. college   a. chief   carrier
2. chief   college
3. carrier

4. teammate   b. aim   teammate
5. aim   flat
6. flat

7. fourth   c. fourth   coach
8. prediction   prediction
9. coach

10. themselves   d. ought   peaceful
11. ought   themselves
12. peaceful

13. mate   e. predict   mate
14. predict

15. imagine   f. imagine
16. imagination   imagination

- - - - - - - - - - - - - - - - - - -

2.

1.	a.	5
	b.	2
	c.	1
	d.	3

2.	a.	1
	b.	3
	c.	2
	d.	3

3.	a.	1
	b.	4
	c.	6
	d.	5

4.	a.	9
	b.	6
	c.	8
	d.	2

B.

17. hard   a. hard   hardship
18. hardship

19. citizen   b. citizen   citizenship
20. citizenship

21. penman   c. penman   penmanship
22. penmanship

23. crime   d. criminal   crime
24. criminal

25. nation   e. nation   national
26. national

27. addition   f. additional   addition
28. additional

C.

	before	at the same time	after
1. whenever	✔		
2. until			✔
3. as		✔	
4. meanwhile		✔	
5. while		✔	

D.

1. peaceful
2. hopeless
3. readable
4. careful
5. quietly
6. politeness
7. slowly
8. sleepless
9. treatable
10. cleverness

CA-27

A.

1.
1. sex   a. pleasant   sex
2. pleasant

3. pulse   b. temperature   pulse
4. temperature

5. cough   c. skin   cough
6. skin

7. infection   d. medicine   infection
8. medicine

9. cure   e. prevent   cure
10. prevent

11. dream   f. appeared   dream
12. appeared

13. dinner   g. bath   dinner
14. comfortable   comfortable
15. bath

16. potato   h. potato   gravy
17. fat   fat
18. gravy

2.

1.	a. 2		2.	a. 4
	b. 3			b. 2
	c. 1			c. 1
	d. 4			d. 3
3.	a. 2		4.	a. 1
	b. 4			b. 4
	c. 1			c. 2
	d. 3			d. 3

B.

19. heal   a. health
20. health

21. sixty   b. sixty
22. sixtieth

23. nine   c. ninth
24. ninth

25. five   d. fifth
26. fifth

27. wide   e. width
28. width

29. deep   f. depth
30. depth

C.

	explains	adds on
a. in other words	✔	
b. also		✔
c. furthermore		✔
d. or		✔
e. for example	✔	
f. such as	✔	

D.

1. mut ter
   a. (short)
   b. (after)
2. re flex
   a. (long)
   b. (short)
3. pun ish
   a. (short)
   b. (wash)
4. en ter tain
   a. (short)
   b. (long)
5. ro man tic
   a. (long)
   b. (short)
   c. (picnic)

CA-28

A.

1.
1. butter
2. bit

a. bit   butter

3. brick
4. cheese

b. cheese   brick

5. wagon
6. cow

c. cow   wagon

7. guide
8. prayer
9. western

d. guide   western
     prayer

10. vegetables
11. ripe

e. vegetables   ripe

12. snake
13. difficult
14. swallow

f. difficult   snake
     swallow

15. mayor
16. decide

g. decide   mayor

17. excites
18. excitement

h. excites   excitement

23. threw
24. weight

e. threw
f. tow

25. tow
26. Bare

g. Bare
h. weight

2.
27. present   29. record
28. desert   30. permit

		Accent on first syllable	Accent on second syllable
i.	record	✔	
j.	desert		✔
k.	present	✔	
l.	Present		✔
m.	desert	✔	
n.	record		✔
o.	permit	✔	
p.	permit		✔

2.

1.			2.		
	a.	1		a.	1
	b.	4		b.	2
	c.	2		c.	3
	d.	3		d.	2

3.			4.		
	a.	1		a.	1
	b.	5		b.	3
	c.	2		c.	4
	d.	4		d.	7

B.

1. 19. witch
20. due

a. due
b. knot

21. eight
22. knot

c. witch
d. eight

C.

	Cause or reason	Effect or result
a. (because)	2	1
b. (therefore)	1	2
c. (thus)	1	2
d. (since)	2	1
e. (so)	1	2

D.

1. rainbow
2. napkins
3. favorite
4. department
5. permission
6. concentrate

CA-29

A.

1.
1. fuse	a. crackle	cord
2. crackle	fuse	
3. cord		

4. plug	b. oil	plug
5. oil		

6. directions	c. visitor	directions
7. visitor		

8. salt	d. screw	salt
9. screw		

10. knife	e. knife	wire
11. wire		

12. flash	f. bunch	flash
13. bunch		

14. quite	g. quite	tight
15. tight		

2.

1.			2.		
	a.	6		a.	3
	b.	3		b.	1
	c.	1		c.	2
	d.	5		d.	5

3.			4.		
	a.	1.2		a.	1
	b.	2.1		b.	4
	c.	1.1		c.	6
	d.	2.2		d.	2

B.

16. decide	debt	a. delicious
17. desert	decide	b. debt
18. delicious	delicious	c. decide
19. debt	desert	d. desert

20. metal	meant	e. medicine
21. medicine	medicine	f. message
22. meant	message	g. meant
23. message	metal	h. metal

24. premium	practice	i. premium
25. prepare	predict	j. predict
26. predict	premium	k. practice
27. practice	prepare	l. prepare

C.

	Contrast	Conclusion
a. in fact	✔	
b. thus		✔
c. so that		✔
d. unlike	✔	
e. but	✔	
f. on the other hand	✔	
g. therefore		✔
h. Rather	✔	

D.

1. salt	6. cough
2. quite	7. knee
3. chief	8. wire
4. knife	9. calm
5. cure	10. tough

CA-30

A.

1.
1. museum   a. several   promise
2. several   museum
3. promise

4. community   b. arena   community
5. arena

6. polio   c. disease   polio
7. disease

8. slave   d. slave   moan
9. cruel   cruel
10. moan

11. clinic   e. x-ray   clinic
12. x-ray

13. guard   f. library   guard
14. library   measles
15. measles

16. thorn   g. limp   thorn
17. limp

- - - - - - - - - - - - - - - - - - - -

2.

1.			2.		
	a.	4		a.	8
	b.	1		b.	3
	c.	2		c.	1
	d.	1		d.	2

3.			4.		
	a.	1.2		a.	1
	b.	1.1		b.	4
	c.	2		c.	2
	d.	2		d.	3

B.

18. paw   a. chest
19. knee   b. paw
20. chest   c. knee
21. skin   d. paw
           e. skin

22. ankle   f. neck
23. finger   g. ankle
24. elbow   h. elbow
25. neck   i. finger

26. stomach   j. hip
27. wrist   k. stomach
28. hip   l. shoulder
29. shoulder   m. stomach
           n. wrist

C.

1.

	Purpose	Condition
a. Whether		✔
b. If		✔
c. unless		✔
d. so that	✔	
e. otherwise		✔

2. a. however   even if   so that
contrast: however   **condition**: even if
purpose: so that

b. Whenever   or   until   and
time: whenever   until
new idea: or   and

c. Since   before   and   too
time: before   **new idea**: and (too)
reason or cause: since

d. Although   and   that is
example: that is   **new idea**: and
contrast: although

D.

1. an kle   4. ex cite ment
2. mu sic   5. dan ger ous
3. in stead   6. in fec tion

Review Lesson
26-30

A.

1. clinic
2. library
3. museum
4. community
5. Chief
6. Several
7. imagine
8. flash
9. practice
10. bath
11. decided
12. moaned
13. metal
14. medicine
15. comfortable
16. fourth
17. difficult
18. delicious
19. cord
20. disease
21. infection
22. arena
23. carriers
24. mayors
25. plug
26. prevent
27. spy
28. guard

The words in the paragraphs are:

clinic community Several imagine
practice decided medicine comfortable
difficult disease infection carriers
prevent guard

B.

29. fat
30. national
31. chest
32. pleasant
33. ankle
34. dinner
35. gravy
36. thorns
37. bricks
38. potatoes
39. salt
40. polio
41. cheese
42. desert
43. cow
44. butter
45. wire
46. vegetables
47. cruel
48. flat
49. aim
50. snake
51. guide
52. promise

The words in the paragraphs are:

fat chest dinner gravy potatoes salt
cheese butter vegetables cruel aim
promise

C.

53. western
54. x-ray
55. bit
56. bunch
57. sex
58. wrist
59. wagons
60. elbows
61. shoulders
62. witches
63. coach
64. mate
65. visitor
66. college
67. Teammates
68. Slaves
69. prediction
70. excitement
71. imagination
72. knife

The words in the paragraphs are:

x-ray bunch wrist elbows shoulders
coach college Teammates excitement
imagination

D.

73. measles
74. screws
75. fuses
76. coughs
77. hardship
78. oil
79. fought
80. ought
81. quite
82. tight
83. appeared
84. repeated
85. swallowed
86. skinned
87. paw
88. pulse
89. finger
90. stomach
91. prayer
92. dream

The words in the paragraphs are:

measles coughs hardship ought quite
appeared swallowed pulse stomach
prayer

E.

93. ripe
94. peaceful
95. temperature
96. crackle
97. nation
98. hip
99. excite
100. predict
101. cure
102. limp
103. themselves
104. direction

The words in the paragraphs are:

peaceful temperature hip predict cure
themselves

EXTENSION ACTIVITY

1. **Choose the word from the box to correctly complete each sentence. Write the word you chose on the blank line.**

toe	plain	ate	fined
tow	plane	eight	find

a. The _____ landed two hours late.

b. Her father bakes very _____ cakes.

c. When the car broke down, they called someone to _____ it away.

d. He stopped playing detective when he fell and hurt his _____ .

e. She was stopped on the highway and _____ for speeding.

f. Children always seem to _____ something to play with.

g. He feeds the children every morning at _____ o'clock.

h. They _____ a large bowl of dry breakfast food.

2. **Fill in the boxes.**

Across

1. very strong
4. better
6. on the other side
8. What is two?

Down

1. large, large hill
2. sells food
3. pull apart
5. someone who uses
7. her

3. **Read the words below. Write each one under the heading where it belongs.**

		Places on Map	Land Forms	Parts of Body
America	blood	_____	_____	_____
bone	Europe	_____	_____	_____
island	mountain	_____	_____	_____
nerves	plain	_____	_____	_____
prairie	states	_____	_____	_____
teeth	towns			

EXTENSION ACTIVITY

1. **Read the sentences below. Write each one on the blank lines, putting in all the marks and big letters that are needed.**

   a. he called the motor vehicle club to ask where he could find a good car

   _____

   _____

   b. we cant help you said the operator

   _____

   c. do you know what i did next asked the man checking the motor

   _____

   _____

   d. nothing you can say will surprise me any more he answered

   _____

   _____

2. **When we break a word into parts or beats, there is one vowel* sound in each part. Read the words below and count the number of parts in each one. Write the number of parts on the blank line. The first one has been done for you.**

   a. difference _3_   e. thunder ____   i. motor ____   m. sharp ____
   b. platform ____   f. vacation ____   j. slender ____   n. service ____
   c. wedding ____   g. vehicle ____   k. challenge ____ o. sandwich ____
   d. condition ____   h. surprise ____   l. understand ____ p. detective ____

3. **Choose a word from the box that has the opposite meaning and write it on the blank line. The first one has been done for you.**

afraid	clear	most	same	soft	untie

   least _most_   hard _____
   different _____   tie _____
   cloudy _____   brave _____

*Ask for help with this word.

EXTENSION ACTIVITY

1. Read the words below. Write each one under the heading where it belongs.

		Furniture	Fishing	Ship
anchor	bait	_____	_____	_____
bed	deck	_____	_____	_____
footstool	hooks	_____	_____	_____
piano	spear	_____	_____	_____

2. When we add the ending <u>ion</u> to a word, we make a new word that is the <u>name</u> of something rather than a statement of <u>what we are doing</u>. Make a new word by adding <u>ion</u> to each word in the box. Write the word you have made in the sentence where it belongs.

> **act   attract   elect   invent**

a. At _____ time, the people running for office give many talks.

b. There was a lot of _____ in the new picture about the Wild West.

c. I think that the dancers were the best _____ of the show.

d. Edison spent a lot of time working on his _____ , the light bulb.

3. Each word below contains 2 small words. Write the small words on the blank lines.

a. clotheshorse _____ _____

b. breakneck _____ _____

c. otherwise _____ _____

d. wisecrack _____ _____

e. repairman _____ _____

f. peacetime _____ _____

g. shipyard _____ _____

h. birthright _____ _____

i. whitefish _____ _____

j. flagship _____ _____

k. ragbag _____ _____

l. alleyway _____ _____

m. penholder _____ _____

n. bridgework _____ _____

o. snowplow _____ _____

p. shadowbox _____ _____

4. Write the word for each number below.

14 _____   16 _____   17 _____

18 _____   19 _____

EXTENSION ACTIVITY

1. **Each word below contains 2 small words. Write the small words on the blank lines.**

   a. rifleman _____ _____   e. shoemaker _____ _____

   b. motorboat _____ _____   f. jailhouse _____ _____

   c. wastepaper _____ _____   g. sharpshooter _____ _____

   d. jailbreak _____ _____   h. uptown _____ _____

2. **Write the word for each number below.**

   60 _____   70 _____   90 _____

3. **Read the words below. Write each one under the heading where it belongs.**

cattle	club	coat	high wind	horses	mouse	puppy	rain
rifle	shoes	slip	snow	spear	suit	sword	thunder

Clothes	Weather	Arms	Animals
_____	_____	_____	_____
_____	_____	_____	_____
_____	_____	_____	_____
_____	_____	_____	_____

4. **Below are some words that sound alike but are not spelled the same, and which have different meanings. Choose the word from the box that correctly completes each sentence. Write the word you chose on the blank line.**

sense	board	threw	meet
cents	bored	through	meat

   a. We usually _____ in the _____ shop.

   b. He had only a few _____ left.

   c. It doesn't make _____ to spend all that money.

   d. We have been _____ all of this before.

   e. She _____ up her hands and left the room.

   f. That _____ is too long and heavy for you to carry alone.

   g. How can anyone be _____ when there are so many good books to read?

EXTENSION ACTIVITY

1. Write the words with the <u>short</u> sound of <u>a</u>, <u>e</u>, <u>i</u>, <u>o</u>, or <u>u</u> under the letter where it belongs. The first one has been done for you.

			a	e	i	o	u
blank	bulb	lick	*blank*	_____	_____	_____	_____
hung	gamble	edge	_____	_____	_____	_____	_____
sick	cut	bell	_____	_____	_____	_____	_____
sense	match	clock	_____	_____	_____	_____	_____
hill	dance	box	_____	_____	_____	_____	_____

2. Draw a line around the sentence that does not belong in the story below. On the blank line above the story, write a good name for the story.

*

_____

The United States is a very beautiful country. There are large grasslands, high green mountains, far-reaching plains, and wonderful waterways. Mrs. Lyndon B. Johnson started a drive to get the people of the United States to help "Keep America Beautiful."

Every year the United States government spends millions of dollars of taxpayers' money to pick up the papers and garbage that are thrown on roads and highways by people in passing cars. Millions of Americans die on our highways every year.

The people who want to work to keep America beautiful find many things they can do. They can try to make their homes prettier. Taking care of homes, painting, and planting things help a lot to make neighborhoods better places in which to live. Just by thinking about throwing things in the places where they belong and doing it, they help keep their homes, their neighborhoods, their cities, and their country more beautiful. They help in the drive to save this country's priceless beauty for today's and tomorrow's Americans.

3. On the blank line, write the words from each box, in order, from the smallest to the largest. The first one has been done for you.

tenth	second	third	first

first, second, third, tenth

thousands	tens	millions	hundreds

_____

hour	month	second	year	day	minute

*Answer will vary.

EXTENSION
ACTIVITY
_____

1. **Each word below contains 2 small words. Write the small words on the blank lines.**

   a. towboat   _____ _____   g. downtown   _____ _____

   b. trainload _____ _____   h. cutthroat   _____ _____

   c. playback   _____ _____   i. clubhouse   _____ _____

   d. bandstand _____ _____   j. churchman   _____ _____

   e. raindrop   _____ _____   k. snowplow   _____ _____

   f. cattlemen _____ _____

2. **When the ending ward is added to a word, it shows the way something is going.**
   "An upward puff of air blew the balloon into the tree."
   Add ward to each word in the box and write it in the sentence where it belongs.

west   back   out

   a. When America was young, there was a large _____ movement.

   b. Why have you put your dress on _____ ?

   c. Although he was sick, there were no _____ signs of illness.

3. **Read the words below and write each one under the heading where it belongs.**

			Days of Week	Army	Factory
Captain	foreman	Friday	_____	_____	_____
General	machines	Monday	_____	_____	_____
Private	Sunday	toolmakers	_____	_____	_____
workers			_____	_____	_____

4. **On the blank line, write each day of the week in the short form. The first one has been done for you.**

   a. Sunday *Sun.*   d. Wednesday _____   g. Saturday _____

   b. Monday _____   e. Thursday _____

   c. Tuesday _____   f. Friday _____

E<small>XTENSION</small>
A<small>CTIVITY</small>

1. Read the words below. Write each one under the heading where it belongs.

		Vehicles	Numbers	Parts of Car
bucket seats	bus	_____	_____	_____
forty	hood	_____	_____	_____
motor	nine	_____	_____	_____
nineteen	sixty	_____	_____	_____
sports car	steering wheel	_____	_____	_____
truck	wheels	_____	_____	_____

2. On the blank line, write a word from the box that tells about each item below.

> who   what   where   when

a. in the alley _____
b. two blankets _____
c. an insurance policy _____
d. thirsty children _____
e. at the factory _____
f. a notice _____
g. a secret _____
h. at that time _____
i. a human being _____
j. last year _____
k. the neighbors _____
l. in the room _____

3. Fill in the boxes.

Across
1. start
4. crying
6. food from a chicken
7. driver of a plane

Down
1. a fight
2. happy
3. fish that didn't get away
5. get money for

EXTENSION ACTIVITY

1. **Draw a line around the sentence that does not belong in the story below.**

George Washington is called the Father of Our Country. Washington lived about two hundred years ago. He was born of rich parents and lived in Virginia.

Before there was a United States of America, this country belonged to England. The people didn't think that it was fair for England to tell them they must pay high taxes and have no voice in the government, so a brave band of men made up their minds to fight the large, strong army of England. Washington wore teeth that were made of wood. George Washington became a General in the army of what later became the United States. He led the men bravely and when it was time to set up a government, he was asked to be the first leader of the new country.

Washington was a good and wise leader and after serving for eight years, he refused to be President any longer. He urged people to remember why they had wanted their own government and to not make one man so strong that he could lead them forever. He judged eight years to be enough for one man to be the President of the United States.

*2. **Write the answer on the blank line to correctly complete each sentence.**

   a. Washington is called the Father of Our Country because _____

   _____ .

   b. The people wanted to fight England because _____

   _____ .

   c. In the new government, Washington was the _____ .

   d. Two hundred years ago this country belonged to _____ .

3. **Cross out the answer that does <u>not</u> belong. The first one has been done for you.**

   a. Washington was called the (Father, ~~Uncle~~) of Our Country.

   b. The men of (England, the United States) won the war.

   c. Washington was a (General, Captain) during the war.

   d. Washington was made President (two, three) times.

*Wording may differ.

1. **Read the words below. Write each one under the heading where it belongs.**

	Business	Groups of People	Sports
bowling boxing	_____	_____	_____
crew crowd	_____	_____	_____
dry cleaners fishing	_____	_____	_____
gang grocery store	_____	_____	_____
pet shop swimming	_____	_____	_____
team TV shop	_____	_____	_____

2. **Below are some words that sound alike but are not spelled the same, and which have different meanings. Choose the word from the box that correctly completes each sentence. Write the word you chose on the blank line.**

bare	weather	do	red
bear	whether	due	read

a. I _____ that book a couple of times.

b. The coat is in the _____ box on the table.

c. I don't remember _____ they came or not.

d. We usually have bad _____ in January.

e. Wouldn't it be wonderful to _____ just the things that interest us?

f. We must remember when the next payment is _____ .

g. The child was shy and hung onto her toy _____ .

h. The little girl's knees were _____ and they looked red and cold.

3. **Choose the word from the box that has the opposite meaning. Write the word you chose on the blank line.**

lie	smart	noise	leave	end	laugh

a. begin _____   d. remain _____

b. truth _____   e. cry _____

c. stupid _____   f. silence _____

CA-25

EXTENSION ACTIVITY

1. Choose the word from the box that has the opposite meaning and write it on the blank line.

| wet | lend | courage | rich | top | best | costly | rested |

a. cheap _____

b. fear _____

c. dry _____

d. bottom _____

e. worst _____

f. poor _____

g. borrow _____

h. tired _____

2. Choose the word from the box that correctly completes each sentence. Write the word you chose on the blank line.

discourage	disinterested	disorderly	distrust
reaction	remain	remarried	reprint
unprepared	unsteady	unusual	unwise

a. He was so ill he had to _____ in the hospital for two weeks.

b. He hadn't walked for so long that when he tried to get up, he was _____ on his feet.

c. She has never _____ since her husband's death.

d. He wanted to be a success so badly that he didn't let anything _____ him.

e. The child was always bored at school and _____ in his lessons.

f. It is _____ to have snow during the month of April.

g. He liked the newspaper story so much that he sent for a _____ to show his friends.

h. He was arrested for _____ conduct.

i. We all _____ him, because he is always telling lies.

j. It is _____ to leave children alone in the house.

k. She had a good _____ to the medicine and felt much better.

l. We were _____ for the test that morning and didn't do well.

112

EXTENSION ACTIVITY

1. **In some words that end in f, we change the f to v and add es to the word to mean more than one. Change the f to v and add es to each word in the box. Write the word you have formed in the sentence where it belongs.**

half   yourself   wolf

   a. You may all help _____ to the cookies and milk.

   b. I cut them up in _____ and saved some for tomorrow.

   c. He told us he had seen _____ in the forest near his cabin.

2. **Read the words below. Write each one under the heading where it belongs.**

	Bodies of Water	Armed Services	On Rulers
army brook	_____	_____	_____
camp discharge	_____	_____	_____
inches ocean	_____	_____	_____
pond river	_____	_____	_____
sailor yard	_____	_____	_____

3. **Make a new word from each word below by writing ful or al on the blank line after the word. Then write the word you have formed in the sentence where it belongs.**

   a. electric_____   c. truth_____   e. cheer_____   g. exception_____

   b. trust_____   d. peace_____   f. government_____

   h. She tried to end their sad meeting on a _____ note.

   i. The child's love of books was truly _____ .

   j. Sometimes it is hard to be _____ and not hurt people's feelings.

   k. He got a job with a _____ agency.

   l. The dog looked at his owner with _____ eyes.

   m. It was cool and _____ in the forest away from everyone.

   n. He opened an _____ repair shop.

4. **On the blank line, write the name of the month in the short form.**

January _____	February _____	March _____
April _____	August _____	September _____
October _____	November _____	December _____

CA-27

EXTENSION ACTIVITY

1. **Make a new word by adding the ending <u>able</u> to each word in the box. Write the word you have formed in the sentence where it belongs.**

> **notice   pay   wash**

a. She always read the tag to see if a new dress was _____ .

b. The notice said that the bill is _____ any time before the 15th.

c. There was a _____ difference between the two colors.

2. **Each word below contains 2 small words. Write the small words on the blank lines.**

a. playmate _____ _____

b. citizenship _____ _____

c. spyglass _____ _____

d. redcoat _____ _____

e. dreamlike _____ _____

f. bathrobe _____ _____

g. nationwide _____ _____

h. handlebars _____ _____

3. **Read the words below. Write each one under the heading where it belongs.**

	Home	Illness	Address
	_____	_____	_____
	_____	_____	_____
	_____	_____	_____
	_____	_____	_____
	_____	_____	_____
	_____	_____	_____

city   closets
dizzy spells   hall
infection   kitchen
living room   sneeze
sore throat   state
street   zone

4. **Make a new word by adding the ending <u>ness</u> to each word below. Write the word you have formed on the blank line.**

a. useful _____

b. dark _____

c. numb _____

d. mad _____

e. great _____

*5. **Write 3 sentences of your own, using one of the new words from Exercise 4 in each sentence.**

a. _____

_____ .

b. _____

_____ .

c. _____

_____ .

*Answers will vary.

EXTENSION ACTIVITY

1. **Write each sentence on the blank lines, putting in all the marks and big letters that are needed.**

   cheese butter and cream can all be made from the milk of a cow

   _____

   _____

   the guide said when you walk in the desert you will not see many snakes

   _____

   _____

   the child asked is it true that some snakes can swallow other animals whole

   _____

   _____

   there are very few of those snakes in our country said the guide you may see them in other places

   _____

   _____

2. **Put this list of job openings in a-b-c order. The first one has been done for you.**

farmer	factory worker	truck driver
policeman	fireman	pilot
roofer	printer	sign painter
nurse	teacher	mailman
telephone operator	foreman	saleswoman
sailor	inventor	manager
prizefighter	doctor	garbage man
detective	businesswoman	

   businesswoman   _____   _____

   _____   _____   _____

   _____   _____   _____

   _____   _____   _____

   _____   _____   _____

   _____   _____   _____

   _____   _____   _____

3. **Choose the word from the box that means the opposite of each word below. Write the word you chose on the blank line.**

illness	able	easy	calm	warlike	fat	front

   a. back _____
   b. thin _____
   c. excited _____
   d. unable _____
   e. health _____
   f. difficult _____
   g. peaceful _____

EXTENSION
ACTIVITY

1. **Read the words below. Then write each one under the heading where it belongs.**

	Tools	Building Materials	Noises
brick crackle	_____	_____	_____
glass grown	_____	_____	_____
metal roar	_____	_____	_____
ruler screwdriver	_____	_____	_____
shovel	_____	_____	_____

2. **When the _less_ ending is added to a word, it usually adds the meaning _without_ to the word's meaning. _Careless_ means _without a care_. When the _ship_ ending is added to a word, it usually means _a state of being_. _Leadership_ means _the state of being a leader_. Make a new word from each word below by writing either _less_ or _ship_ on the blank line. Then write the word you have formed in the sentence where it belongs. The first one has been done for you.**

a. hope _less_   b. pain _____   c. care _____   d. point _____

e. hard _____   f. friend_____   g. court _____   h. leader _____

i. After a short _____ , they were married.

j. The whole talk seemed boring and _____ .

k. The boys' _____ started when they were children in school.

l. She is very sick; the doctors say her case is _hopeless_ .

m. Don't you think she is getting _____ about the way she looks?

n. He gave the city good _____ after he was elected to office.

o. The doctor gave him a shot, and he was surprised that it was completely

_____ .

p. It was a _____ for her to care for an extra child.

3. **Each word below contains 2 small words. Write the small words on the blank lines.**

a. flashlight   _____ _____   g. mountaintop _____ _____

b. oilskin   _____ _____   h. saltwater   _____ _____

c. thumbscrew _____ _____   i. cheesecake   _____ _____

d. guidebook   _____ _____   j. overripe   _____ _____

e. flashbulb   _____ _____   k. watermark   _____ _____

f. rattlesnake   _____ _____   l. surefire   _____ _____

CA-30

EXTENSION
ACTIVITY

1. **Some words ending in y change the y to i and add er. Make a new word for each word in the box by changing the y to i and adding er. Write the word you have formed in the sentence where it belongs. The first one has been done for you.**

fly	early	busy	heavy

a. The *flier* landed his plane in the field.

b. The fighter was _____ than we expected him to be.

c. The train arrived _____ than usual.

d. In our office, we are _____ than usual these days.

2. **On the blank line, write a word from the box that tells about each item below.**

who	what	when	where

a. polio shots _____   g. several days later _____

b. at the library _____   h. in the community _____

c. older citizens _____   i. on Saturday _____

d. at the museum _____   j. every six months _____

e. in childhood _____   k. a childhood disease _____

f. in the library _____   l. the young people _____

3. **Choose the word from the box that has the opposite meaning of each word below and write it on the blank line.**

adult	bury	famous	fear	foggy	lose	loudly	love	proud	yours

a. clear _____   f. gain _____

b. hate _____   g. child _____

c. courage _____   h. unknown _____

d. mine _____   i. faintly _____

e. ashamed _____   j. dig up _____

4. **Read the words below. Write each one under the heading where it belongs.**

	Buildings	Electric	Parts of Body
cheek church	_____	_____	_____
factory grocery store	_____	_____	_____
light bulb mouth	_____	_____	_____
radio throat	_____	_____	_____
tongue TV	_____	_____	_____

117

CA-16

1. a. plane
   b. plain
   c. tow
   d. toe
   e. fined
   f. find
   g. eight
   h. ate

2.

¹m	i	²g	h	³t	y
o	■	r	■	e	■
u	■	o	■	a	■
⁴n	i	c	e	r	■
t	■	e	■	■	⁵u
⁶a	c	r	o	⁷s	s
i	■	■	■	h	e
⁸n	u	m	b	e	r

3.

Places on Map	Land Forms	Parts of Body
America	island	blood
Europe	mountain	bone
states	plain	nerves
towns	prairie	teeth

CA-17

1. a. He called the Motor Vehicle Club to ask where he could find a good car.
   b. "We can't help you," said the operator.
   c. "Do you know what I did next?" asked the man, checking the motor.
   d. "Nothing you can say will surprise me any more," he answered.

2.

	e. 2	i. 2	m. 1
b. 2	f. 3	j. 2	n. 2
c. 2	g. 3	k. 2	o. 2
d. 3	h. 2	l. 3	p. 3

3.

	soft
same	untie
clear	afraid

CA-18

1.

Furniture	Fishing	Ship
bed	bait	anchor
footstool	hooks	deck
piano	spear	

2. a. election
   b. action
   c. attraction
   d. invention

3. a. clothes   horse
   b. break   neck
   c. other   wise
   d. wise   crack
   e. repair   man
   f. peace   time
   g. ship   yard
   h. birth   right
   i. white   fish
   j. flag   ship
   k. rag   bag
   l. alley   way
   m. pen   holder
   n. bridge   work
   o. snow   plow
   p. shadow   box

4. fourteen   sixteen   seventeen
   eighteen   nineteen

CA-19

1. a. rifle   man   e. shoe   maker
   b. motor   boat   f. jail   house
   c. waste   paper   g. sharp   shooter
   d. jail   break   h. up   town

2. sixty   seventy   ninety

3.

Clothes	Weather	Arms	Animals
coat	highwind	club	cattle
shoes	rain	rifle	horses
slip	snow	spear	mouse
suit	thunder	sword	puppy

4. a. meet   neat
   b. cents
   c. sense
   d. through
   e. threw
   f. board
   g. bored

CA-20

1.

a	e	i	o	u
	bell	lick	box	bulb
match	edge	hill	clock	hung
dance	sense	sick		cut
gamble				

2. Millions of Americans die on our highways every year.

3. tens, hundreds, thousands, millions
   second, minute, hour, day, month, year

CA-21

1. a. tow   boat   g. down   town
   b. train   load   h. cut   throat
   c. play   back   i. club   house
   d. band   stand   j. church man
   e. rain   drop   k. snow   plow
   f. cattle   men

2. a. westward
   b. backward
   c. outward

3.

Days of Week	Army	Factory
Friday	Captain	foreman
Monday	General	machines
Sunday	Private	toolmakers
		workers

4. a. Sun.   d. Wed.   g. Sat.
   b. Mon.   e. Thurs.
   c. Tues.   f. Fri.

CA-22

1.

Vehicles	Numbers	Parts of a Car
bus	forty	bucket seats
sports car	nine	hood
truck	nineteen	motor
	sixty	steering wheel
		wheels

2.
a. where g. what
b. what   h. when
c. what   i. who
d. who   j. when
e. where k. who
f. what   l. where

3.

	b	e	g	i	n		c
	a		l				a
	t	e	a	r	s		u
	t		d		e	g	g
	l				l		h
	e		p	i	l	o	t

CA-23

1. Washington wore teeth that were made of wood.

2. a. he served as the first leader of the new country.
b. England was making them pay high taxes
c. President
d. England

3. b. England
c. Captain
d. three

CA-24

1.

Businesses	Groups of People	Sports
dry cleaners	crew	bowling
grocery store	crowd	boxing
pet shop	gang	fishing
TV shop	team	swimming

2.
a. read
b. red
c. whether
d. weather
e. do
f. due
g. bear
h. bare

3. a. end   d. leave
b. lie   e. laugh
c. smart f. noise

CA-25

1. a. costly   e. best
b. courage f. rich
c. wet   g. legend
d. top   h. rested

2. a. remain
b. unsteady
c. remarried
d. discourage
e. disinterested
f. unusual
g. reprint
h. disorderly
i. distrust
j. unwise
k. reaction
l. unprepared

CA-26

1. a. yourselves
b. halves
c. wolves

2.

Bodies of Water	Armed Services	On Rulers
brook	army	inches
ocean	camp	yard
pond	discharge	
river	sailor	

3. a. al   c. ful   e. ful   g. al
b. ful   d. ful   f. al
h. cheerful
i. exceptional
j. truthful
k. governmental
l. trustful
m. peaceful
n. electrical

4. Jan.   Feb.   Mar.
Apr.   Aug.   Sept.
Oct.   Nov.   Dec.

CA-27

1. a. washable
b. payable
c. noticable

2.
a. play   mate   e. dream   like
b. citizen ship   f. bath   room
c. spy   glass   g. nation   wide
d. red   coat   h. handle   bars

3.

Home	Illness	Address
closets	dizzy spells	city
hall	infection	state
kitchen	sneeze	street
living room	sore throat	zone

4. a. usefulness   d. madness
b. darkness   e. greatness
c. numbness

5. Answers will vary.

CA-28

1. Cheese, butter, and cream can all be made from the milk of a cow.
The guide said, "When you walk in the desert, you will not see many snakes."
The child asked, "Is it true that some snakes can swallow other animals whole?"
"There are very few of those snakes in our country," said the guide. "You may see them in other places."

2.

businesswoman	foreman	pilot	saleswoman
detective	garbage man	policeman	sign painter
doctor	inventor	printer	teacher
factory worker	mailman	prizefighter	telephone operator
farmer	manager	roofer	truck driver
fireman	nurse	sailor	

3.
a. front   d. able
b. fat   e. illness
c. calm   f. easy
            g. warlike

CA-29

1.

Tools	Building Materials	Noises
ruler	brick	crackle
screwdriver	glass	growl
shovel	metal	roar
	wood	

2.
            b. less   c. less   d. less
e. ship   f. ship   g. ship   h. ship
i. courtship
j. pointless
k. friendship
l. hopeless
m. careless
n. leadership
o. painless
p. hardship

3.
a. flash light   g. mountain top
b. oil   skin   h. salt   water
c. thumb screw   i. cheese   cake
d. guide book   j. over   ripe
e. flash bulb   k. water   mark
f. rattle snake   l. sure   fire

CA-30

1. b. heavier
     c. earlier
     d. busier

2. a. what   g. when
     b. where   h. where
     c. who   i. when
     d. where   j. when
     e. when   k. what
     f. where   l. who

3. a. foggy   f. lose
     b. love   g. adult
     c. fear   h. famous
     d. yours   i. loudly
     e. proud   j. bury

4.

Buildings	Electric	Parts of Body
church	light bulb	cheek
factory	radio	mouth
grocery store	TV	throat
		tongue

Lesson No.	A — Lesson Skill	Date	Mastery Level	Score	Score	B — Lesson Skill	Date	Mastery Level	Score
			Dictionary Study						
16	Words in sentences; dictionary study	——	$\frac{8}{11}$	$\overline{11}$	$\overline{16}$	Alphabetical order	——	$\frac{14}{18}$	$\overline{18}$
17	Words in sentences; dictionary study	——	$\frac{10}{13}$	$\overline{13}$	$\overline{16}$	Sentence types: statements, questions, exclamations, and commands	——	$\frac{9}{12}$	$\overline{12}$
18	Words in sentences; dictionary study	——	$\frac{9}{12}$	$\overline{12}$	$\overline{16}$	The suffix *ish*	——	$\frac{9}{12}$	$\overline{12}$
19	Words in sentences; dictionary study	——	$\frac{8}{10}$	$\overline{10}$	$\overline{16}$	Alphabetical order: second-, third-, and fourth-letter discrimination	——	$\frac{16}{20}$	$\overline{20}$
20	Words in sentences; dictionary study	——	$\frac{8}{16}$	$\overline{16}$	$\overline{16}$	The prefix *re*	——	$\frac{9}{12}$	$\overline{12}$
	Review Lesson 16–20	——	$\frac{38}{47}$	$\overline{47}$					
21	Words in sentences; dictionary study	——	$\frac{13}{16}$	$\overline{16}$	$\overline{16}$	Compound words	——	$\frac{10}{13}$	$\overline{13}$
22	Words in sentences; dictionary study	——	$\frac{14}{18}$	$\overline{18}$	$\overline{16}$	Compound words: numbers and family relationships	——	$\frac{9}{12}$	$\overline{12}$
23	Words in sentences; dictionary study	——	$\frac{11}{14}$	$\overline{14}$	$\overline{16}$	Synonyms and antonyms	——	$\frac{8}{11}$	$\overline{11}$
24	Words in sentences; dictionary study	——	$\frac{8}{11}$	$\overline{11}$	$\overline{16}$	The calendar	——	$\frac{15}{19}$	$\overline{19}$
25	Words in sentences; dictionary study	——	$\frac{8}{11}$	$\overline{11}$	$\overline{16}$	The prefix *un* and initial *a*	——	$\frac{9}{12}$	$\overline{12}$
	Review Lesson 21–25	——	$\frac{42}{52}$	$\overline{52}$					
26	Words in sentences; dictionary study	——	$\frac{13}{16}$	$\overline{16}$	$\overline{16}$	The suffixes *ship* and *al*	——	$\frac{9}{12}$	$\overline{12}$
27	Words in sentences; dictionary study	——	$\frac{14}{18}$	$\overline{18}$	$\overline{16}$	The suffix *th*	——	$\frac{5}{6}$	$\overline{6}$
28	Words in sentences; dictionary study	——	$\frac{14}{18}$	$\overline{18}$	$\overline{16}$	Homonyms and homographs	——	$\frac{19}{24}$	$\overline{24}$
29	Words in sentences; dictionary study	——	$\frac{12}{15}$	$\overline{15}$	$\overline{16}$	Alphabetical order	——	$\frac{19}{24}$	$\overline{24}$
30	Words in sentences; dictionary study	——	$\frac{14}{17}$	$\overline{17}$	$\overline{16}$	The parts of the body	——	$\frac{11}{14}$	$\overline{14}$
	Review Lesson 26–30	——	$\frac{42}{52}$	$\overline{52}$					

Progress Chart

Language Skills | Spelling

C — Lesson/Skill	Date	Mastery Level	Score	D — Lesson/Skill	Date	Mastery Level	Score	Lesson Words Date	Mastery Level	Score	Review Score
Response utterances	___	6/8	8	Sounds of *y*	___	9/12	12	___	16/20	20	10
Not and negative sentence	___	5/6	6	Syllables	___	8/10	10	___	17/21	21	10
Question markers	___	5/6	6	Dividing words between consonants	___	16/20	20	___	14/18	18	10
Questions: helping word reversals	___	8/10	10	Closed syllables and short vowel sounds	___	8/10	10	___	14/18	18	10
Question markers *do* and *don't*	___	4/5	5	Dividing words with digraphs and blends	___	5/6	6	___	14/18	18	10
Prepositional phrases	___	29/36	36	Dividing words with a first vowel followed by a single consonant (be/cause)	___	8/10	10	___	16/20	20	10
Active and passive sentences	___	22/28	28	Open and closed syllables	___	11/14	14	___	17/21	21	10
Connectives	___	12/15	15	Dividing words with a first vowel followed by a single consonant (nev/er)	___	8/10	10	___	18/19	19	10
Conjunctions	___	4/5	5	Dividing words that end in a consonant before *le*	___	8/10	10	___	18/22	22	19
Pronoun referents	___	16/20	20	Prefixes *un*, *re*, and *dis*	___	8/10	10	___	15/19	19	10
Embedded sentences: conjunctions which show *time reference*	___	4/5	5	Suffixes: *ful*, *less*, *ness*, *ly*, and *able*	___	8/10	10	___	14/18	18	10
Embedded sentences: conjunctions which show *examples* or *additional thought*	___	5/6	6	Unlocking syllables	___	13/16	16	___	14/18	18	10
Embedded sentences: *cause* and *effect* (reason and result)	___	8/10	10	Unlocking new words	___	4/6	6	___	16/20	20	10
Embedded sentences: conjunctions which show *contrast* and *conclusion*	___	13/16	16	Using the dictionary pronunciation guide	___	8/10	10	___	14/18	18	10
Embedded sentences: conjunctions which show *condition* and *purpose*, summary of use of conjunctions	___	26/32	32	Accented syllables	___	4/6	6	___	20/25	25	10

Pronunciation Key

How to say each word is shown just after the word, in this way:

        ab•bre•vi•ate (ə brē′ vē āt).

The letters and signs used are pronounced as in the words below.

The mark ′ is placed after a syllable with primary or heavy accent, as in the example above.

The mark ′ after a syllable shows a secondary or lighter accent, as in

        ab•bre•vi•a•tion (ə brē′ vē ā′ shən).

a	hat, cap		p	paper, cup
ā	age, face		r	run, try
ä	father, far		s	say, yes
			sh	she, rush
b	bad, rob		t	tell, it
ch	child, much		th	thin, both
d	did, red		ᵺ	then, smooth
e	let, best		u	cup, butter
ē	equal, be		u̇	full, put
ėr	term, learn		ü	rule, mule
f	fat, if		v	very, save
g	go, bag		w	will, woman
h	he, how		y	young, yet
			z	zero, breeze
i	it, pin		zh	measure, seizure
ī	ice, five			
			ə	represents:
j	jam, enjoy			a in about
k	kind, seek			e in taken
l	land, coal			i in pencil
m	me, am			o in lemon
n	no, in			u in circus
ng	long, bring			
o	hot, rock			
ō	open, go			
ô	order, all			
oi	oil, voice			
ou	house, out			